Messianic Jews

CHALLENGING CHURCH AND SYNAGOGUE

Messianic Jews

CHALLENGING CHURCH AND SYNAGOGUE

John Fieldsend

MARC
OLIVE PRESS

British Library Cataloguing in Publication Data
A catalogue record for this book is available
from the British Library.

ISBN 1 85424 228 8

Biblical quotations are from the
New International Version © 1973, 1978, 1984 by the
International Bible Society

Production and Printing in England for
MONARCH PUBLICATIONS
PO Box 163, Tunbridge Wells
Kent TN3 0NZ by
Nuprint Ltd, Station Road, Harpenden, Herts, AL5 4SE

Contents

Acknowledgements

I WOULD WISH TO THANK those who have shared their life stories with me for inclusion in this book, and in so doing have shared much of themselves. My thanks are also gratefully offered to Rev Dr Walter Riggans for many helpful comments on the manuscript; it may sometimes be glaringly obvious that I have not always followed it, and I would not wish him to be held responsible for my shortcomings.

I am truly grateful for the understanding of our Messianic Fellowship 'Beth Shalom' for their patience in my distractions from the care and leadership they deserve.

Most of all, I dedicate this book to Elizabeth, without whose unfailing love and support the writing of this book would not have been achieved.

Introduction

T HIS BOOK IS not just about doctrine or theology, but about a living movement. We cannot describe a movement in isolation; we have to see it both in relationship with, and in distinction from, those movements with which it has links. The movement of the Holy Spirit among Jewish people, revealing Jesus as the long awaited Messiah, can only be understood in the context of its relationship with, its distinction from, and its distinctiveness within those communities within which it was born and functions and with which it relates, namely Christianity and Judaism. So in describing and understanding Messianic Judaism we shall have to look not only at its own historic growth but also its relationships with and within both Judaism and Christianity.

What is Messianic Judaism? Is it something really progressive, or, as some may fear, a regression into legalism? These are valid questions, and they are being vigorously debated within the movement itself, where we have to acknowledge a broad variety of opinion.

A quick, rough and ready description would see Hebrew Christianity as the fruit of Christian missionary activity, bringing Jewish people to faith in Jesus as Saviour and Messiah, building them up into full membership of the Church, and bringing them into membership of one of the historic denominations, accepting that they also share a fellowship one with another in their Jewish identity. On the other hand Messianic Judaism sees itself as an indigenous movement within the body of Messiah, one in faith with their Gentile brothers and sisters, and yet maintaining congregational autonomy and independence.

I shall use the word 'Gentile' throughout this book in the biblical sense of 'those other than Jews': it carries with it no undertones of 'pagan'. The context will make clear whether Gentile Christians or Gentile unbelievers are being referred to.

There are inevitably tensions within the whole movement

which are still being worked out, and which create tensions also in our relationship with the historic churches. Some of these will be examined in the course of this book.

My own perspective is that the difference between Messianic Judaism and Hebrew Christianity is real, but it is one of natural development rather than fundamental. I am happy to be described by either title, though being part of the flow of this present history, I have to say that I prefer Messianic Judaism as a more accurate description of where 'we are at' to use current jargon. Also my position is that while I recognise the independence of Messianic Congregations, and in fact have a pastoral eldership role within one, I am also an ordained minister of the Church of England. I would therefore naturally want to emphasise the essential unity we have with other churches, and I have no difficulty with calling myself a Christian.

I can, however, understand those of my fellow members of the Messianic Jewish movement who may be the only believer in an otherwise wholly Jewish family. While seeing themselves fully one in faith with non Jewish members of the body of Messiah they may prefer not to call themselves Christians because of the misunderstanding this causes in their families and the wider Jewish community. They are not ashamed of the name of Christ, but they do want, rightly, to witness to the essential Jewishness of Jesus and the faith of those who follow him. Before non Jewish Christians criticise them for what may seem like a spirit of separatism, let them reflect deeply that the need for this seeming soft pedalling, not of the name of the Messiah, but rather of the Church that bears his name, is the history of antisemitism. This is something that the church has never been totally clear of, and which at times seems to have been almost endemic; and following that reflection, perhaps to understand and support. These are not our 'weaker' brethren; they are perhaps our strongest.

When we ask 'What's in a name?' it is important not only to ask 'What are we seeking to convey?' but more importantly 'What do those with whom we are seeking to communicate, understand?' Where others do not understand, we have not taught.

Central to the book are three chapters relating to our understanding of The Acts of the Apostles and Paul's Letters to the

Romans and Galatians, especially as they impinge on the relationship of Jewish and Gentile believers in Jesus. We shall also look at the variety of understanding within Judaism throughout its history, regarding the person and work of the Messiah. If Messianic Judaism is to stand the test of integrity, it must show its credentials as valid, both biblically, and from the standpoint of the traditions of Judaism. But this is not just a theological or an historical book: it is also a book about people. Integral to the book therefore are the stories of Jewish people who have come to believe that Jesus is the Messiah. Some, for very real reasons are giving their story under a 'nom de plume'. But they are all people I know well, and we have spent many hours together preparing this book. I can vouch for the integrity of what they have contributed.

CHAPTER 1

Come Worship with Us

A GROUP OF PEOPLE are gathering together in a flat in north London. Greetings are exchanged, there is the lively chatter of friends catching up on the past week's happenings. A guitar and other instruments are tuned, and after the refreshments are cleared away a time of worship, teaching and sharing begins. You might say that there is nothing particularly new in all that. House groups, prayer cells, house churches etc are increasingly a part of the Christian scene in the second half of this century. The group we are about to join is part of that scene, and yet it is somehow different.

The time is 10.30 on a Saturday morning, and apart from Seventh Day Adventist groups, not many Christian groups gather on that day or at that time. Some of the songs are well known, others in a foreign language. The Scripture readings, though familiar, are announced as from the Torah, the HafTorah or the Brit hadashah.[1] Much of the worship is extempore, but there are also some beautiful prayers adapted from a prayer book called the *Siddur*.[2] At one point the assembled company stands, not to recite the creed, but to sing the Shema, 'Shema Israel, Adonai Eloheynu Adonai Echad...Hear O Israel, the Lord our God, the Lord is One...'. The worship concludes with a Communion service with a very clear Passover theme running through it. Notices for the coming weeks include an invitation from another fellowship in north-east London inviting them to share in their Purim Party, to celebrate the events recorded in the Book of Esther. Further brief discussion finalises the details for the Pesach Seder (Passover Meal and Celebration). They then share in a very pleasant buffet lunch provided by their host, a young solicitor whose story you will read later in this book.

This is one of the growing number of Messianic Congregations or Fellowships that are springing up in most places where there is a Jewish community. Of the fifteen people present, twelve are Jewish and three are Gentiles who value sharing in the life and worship of such a group. The Jewish members are from a great variety of backgrounds. Some come from a life of Jewish orthodoxy; others from a more liberal background. Some from years of Jewish religious practice; others from a more secular lifestyle. This should not be surprising, since religious practice in Judaism today is as varied as in Christianity, and the proportion of secularised, non-practising Jews are as high as in the parallel Gentile culture.

The worship and teaching are certainly Jewish in ethos. Interested Jewish visitors, used to a synagogue service, would not have felt out of place, but Jesus is fully honoured as Messiah, Saviour and Lord. As a matter of fact, Jesus is normally called 'Yeshua' (Joshua), and why not? After all, that was the name given at his circumcision!

At the time of writing there are three Messianic fellowships or congregations in the London area, and about a dozen scattered throughout the British Isles. In Israel there are about forty, some worshipping totally in Hebrew, some in English and others in Russian. In the USA the number runs into hundreds, and there are others wherever there are Jewish communities, including South America and South Africa. The opening up of Eastern Europe has shown that not only has Christianity survived the years of communist oppression, but also that Jewish people have come to faith in Jesus as their Messiah. There are Messianic congregations in the previous USSR, in Poland and elsewhere. The congregations vary in size, ethos and doctrinal emphasis, but they have in common a desire to express a biblically based belief in Yeshua as Messiah and Saviour. In some congregations there is a greater emphasis on 'Halakah'[3] – which is basically the Oral Law, the accepted rabbinic tradition of interpretation of the Written Law, whilst others would see this as a less important part of a biblical expression of their Judaism.

Messianic Judaism is a broad based movement. For some Messianic Jews the memory of Church based antisemitism is so great that Christian terminology and tradition is suspect. Others, whilst focusing on the particular ethos of Messianic Judaism, find no problem, without being blinkered to history, in identifying with the Church.

These are matters of ongoing debate within the Messianic Movement. Other differences of emphasis have, regrettably, been imported from the surrounding churches, such as the charismatic issue, etc. As regards the practice of baptism, most congregations would practise believers' baptism. This causes some surprise amongst adherents of those historic churches that practise infant baptism, because the link with infant circumcision has been traditionally one of the main supports for that practice. However our reasoning is that circumcision is a sign of what we already are—Jewish by birth. Our baptism is a sign of what we have become by new birth, children of God through faith in Yeshua our Messiah. We do not see baptism either replacing or 'fulfilling' circumcision: each in its own right expresses a different aspect of our identity. Many Messianic families still have their male babies circumcised, while baptism generally awaits their personal declaration of faith. It is worth noting that Paul had Timothy circumcised, even though presumably he would already have been baptised: his baptism expressed his membership of the universal Body of Messiah, Jew and Gentile together; his circumcision expressed his membership of God's historic covenant people, the Jewish people. The view that baptism has replaced circumcision as the sign of initiation into the people of God seems to many of us to be an expression of that error in much of historic Christianity which we shall come up against again and again—Replacement Theology—whereby the Church is seen as replacing the Jewish people as the people of God.

WORSHIP AND HISTORY

One difference between Jewish and Christian worship is that while Christians focus almost exclusively on the historic event that brought salvation into the world—the incarnation, death and resurrection of Jesus—Jewish worship incorporates much more the stories of the many deliverances God has wrought for his people throughout their history. This may be a simplistic over-statement to make a point, but nevertheless it conveys one real difference between the ethos of Christian and Jewish spirituality.

Not that history is unimportant to Christians. But apart from the period of biblical history, especially the period of New Testament history, and more particularly the events that related to the passion of Jesus, the rest of Christian history does not feature very much in Church worship.

A Purim party we attended was particularly interesting. The story of Esther was acted out, mainly by children, with just one or two parts taken by adults. In keeping with tradition, there was much hissing, booing, stamping of feet and the noise of football rattles, every time the name of Haman, the villain of the plot, was mentioned. But what made this production stand out was that it was spoken entirely in Hebrew, with an English translation given by quite a young girl. For Jewish people the Feast of Esther is not just part of our ancient history. It is that, of course, but much more. The drama of the festival centres on Esther 3:8-11.

> Then Haman said to King Xerxes, 'There is a certain people dispersed and scattered among the peoples in all the provinces of your kingdom whose customs are different from those of all other people and who do not obey the king's laws; it is not in the king's best interest to tolerate them. If it pleases the king, let a decree be issued to destroy them, and I will put ten thousand talents of silver into the royal treasury for the men who carry out this business.' So the king took his signet ring from his finger and gave it to Haman son of Hammedatha, the Agagite, the enemy of the Jews. 'Keep the money,' the king said to Haman, 'and do with the people as you please.'

In our history there have been many Hamans, and in this century the Shoah (Shoah is the preferable term for what has been called the Holocaust, because Holocaust is the technical biblical word for a voluntary whole burnt sacrifice, where Shoah carries with it the thought of total destruction) more nearly achieved Haman's ambitions than any other catastrophe in our history. I have heard it put it like this. The inquisition stated 'You cannot live amongst us as Jews, so convert!' The pogroms stated 'You cannot live amongst us, so go somewhere else.' Hitler stated simply 'You cannot live.'

Messianic Jewish worship seeks to marry the best of both traditions, in that Jewish history, not just biblical history, is our history. Other similar events, not just the events related in the book of Esther; the Crusades, the Inquisition, the Pogroms, the Shoah and the rebuilding of a homeland in Eretz Israel, are part of our experience.

Let the reader be in no doubt that Messianic Jewish worship certainly centres fully on the unique and sufficient sacrifice of Yeshua as the one complete and sufficient atonement sacrifice for our sins. That is absolutely non-negotiable.

At that Purim party there were many guests, both Jewish and Gentile, whose lives were not yet committed to Jesus as Saviour and Lord, and I had the great privilege of speaking evangelistically of a greater deliverance that God has worked, not of deliverance from human opposition, but from the bondage to sin. But because we Jews are all members of one historic people, the story of our peoplehood, and the story of God's action seen in our joys and in our sorrows, in our experiences of God's discipline and God's mighty acts of deliverance in solid history, is different from the way Gentile Christians normally look at biblical history.

WORSHIP AND FESTIVALS

Many Christians express concern, frequently open opposition, when Messianic Jews incorporate the Jewish festivals into their worship. One notable exception is the Passover, for this has clear Christian connotations.

> Get rid of the old yeast that you may be a new batch without yeast–as you really are. For Christ, our Passover lamb, has been sacrificed. Therefore let us keep the Festival, not with the old yeast, the yeast of malice and wickedness, but with bread without yeast, the bread of sincerity and truth. (1 Cor 5:7,8).

It has become acceptable, even enthusiastically fashionable, for churches to re-enact the Passover during Holy Week, but the danger is that it is not accepted as something in its own right for Jewish people, but as something that has been 'baptised' for Christians as bringing out the deeper significance of the Last Supper. The latter is indeed true, but it does not have to deny Messianic Jews the former.

As regards Pentecost, many Christians do not even realise that this is a Jewish festival, and somehow Tabernacles has not been 'christianised' into the calendar of the Church's year, though many Christians whose teaching contains a strong prophetic element regarding Israel now see great significance in the festival, with special reference to Zechariah 14:16

> Then the survivors from all the nations that have attacked Jerusalem will go up year after year to worship the King, the LORD Almighty, and to celebrate the Feast of Tabernacles.

The reason for Christian reservation about Messianic Jews celebrating these festivals is that it might bring us back under bondage to the law. That caution is expressed most strongly when we celebrate what are perceived to be non-biblical aspects of those festivals. Certainly we would strongly affirm the difference between biblical Judaism and rabbinic Judaism, and our concern to follow the former. This is something that will be highlighted throughout this book, but we shall also note that Jesus did not make, as is frequently assumed in the Church, a blanket condemnation of the rabbis; indeed we shall look into the probability that he lived and ministered as one of them.

We shall now look at Jesus' attitude to the Jewish festivals and let that be the basis of our practice. Let us take the Feast of Dedication, John 10:22-25, as our first example.

> Then came the Feast of Dedication at Jerusalem. It was winter, and Jesus was in the temple area walking in Solomon's Colonnade. The Jews gathered round him, saying, 'How long will you keep us in suspense? If you are the Christ, tell us plainly.' Jesus answered, 'I did tell you, but you do not believe. The miracles I do in my Father's name speak for me,...

We should note that this is not one of the biblical festivals. The occasion celebrated is the purification and rededication of the Temple after the victory of Judas Maccabeus over Antiochus IVth. Tradition has it that for the rededication God performed a 'great miracle' in that one day's supply of oil lasted seven days. Hence Jesus not only celebrated the festival, he used it to challenge the people to recognise that his miracles were his authentication.

Next let us look at the way Jesus kept and used the Festival of Sukkot (Tabernacles) in John 7 and 8.

> On the last and greatest day of the Feast, Jesus stood and said in a loud voice, 'If anyone is thirsty, let him come to me and drink. (Jn 7:37).

> When Jesus spoke again to the people, he said, 'I am the light of the world. Whoever follows me will never walk in darkness, but will have the light of life.' (Jn 8:12)

We need to understand that in the biblical record of the Old Testament, Sukkot was entirely a harvest centred festival. The themes of Water and Light became very much part of the priestly oral tradition, yet Jesus obviously felt quite at home in participating in the Temple festival and focusing these traditions upon himself. If Jesus so celebrated and used the rabbinic elements in these festivals as signs proclaiming his Messianic identity, may not we, his Jewish followers do the same?

If it be said that these things all took place before the resurrection and the founding of the New Testament Church, then we will point to the consistent practice of Paul, who also maintained his observance of the Jewish festivals and ceremonies, as did other Jewish followers of Jesus.

I am not suggesting that these festivals, in their Jewish context, should become festivals for the whole Church. However, for us as Messianic Jews, these festivals, and the events they celebrate, are a part of our real history, records of the mighty works of God on our behalf. Should it then seem unreasonable to our Gentile brothers and sisters in Christ that they continue to play an important part in our worship? Yet this is something we frequently have to justify, though not perhaps in the extreme form found in the *Profession from the Church of Constantinople* which Jews had to affirm if they wanted to join the Church.

> I renounce all customs, rites, legalisms, unleavened breads and sacrifices of lambs of the Hebrews, and all other feasts of the Hebrews, sacrifices, prayers, aspersions, purifications, sanctifications and propitiations, and fasts and new moons, and sabbaths, and superstitions, and hymns and chants and observances and synagogues, and the food and drink of the Hebrews; in one word, I

renounce absolutely everything Jewish, every law, rite and custom...and if afterwards I shall wish to deny and return to Jewish
superstition, or be found eating with Jews, or feasting with them,
or secretly conversing and condemning the Christian religion
instead of openly confuting them and condemning their vain faith,
then let the trembling of Cain and the leprosy of Gehazi cleave to
me, as well as the legal punishments to which I acknowledge
myself liable. And may I be anathema in the world to come, and
may my soul be set down with Satan and the devils.[4]

It would be easy to shrug this off as an ancient response by a
Church which is no longer representative of living Christianity as
we know it today. However, I know of too many Messianic Jews
who have been put under great pressure to give up their keeping
of Jewish festivals if they are to be accepted into church membership, and I know how many times my own observation of them
has caused raised eyebrows and serious questionings and reserva-
tions within the recognised church leadership.

Another tension for Messianic believers is the separation
between the observance of Passover and Easter caused by the
redating of Easter at the Council of Nicea in 325 CE (Common
Era–a term more acceptable than AD to Jewish people–and in
the place of BC we shall use BCE–before the Common Era).
Whatever the reason was for this action, its result was that Jewish
believers in Jesus were faced with pressure to drop their Passover
observance if they were to celebrate Easter in the Church. It is
natural and right that Messianic Jews should wish to maintain
the direct calendar link between the death of Jesus and the
sacrifice of the Passover lambs. This causes a separation of the
remembrance from our Gentile Christian friends, sometimes by
several weeks. Often we are accused of being separatist; whereas
it was the Gentile dominated Council of Nicea that originated the
break. This of course has a knock-on effect on the dating of
Pentecost fifty days later.

One looks with hope at the possibility of a deepening understanding on the part of Gentile Christians for the integrity and
value of Messianic congregations and their observance of these
festivals. They have not been created out of a spirit of divisiveness
or a sense of superiority, but as an expression of what God has
done for us and in us. We would not expect our Gentile brothers

and sisters in Christ to incorporate them into their worship and lifestyle, and we hope they would not expect us to give them up as no longer relevant to someone whose faith is in Jesus our Messiah. After all, he was part of our national experience, though we were not aware of it, over a thousand years before the incarnation. As Paul explicitly states in 1 Corinthians 10:1-4.

> For I do not want you to be ignorant of the fact, brothers, that our forefathers were all under the cloud and that they all passed through the sea. They were all baptised into Moses in the cloud and in the sea. They all ate the same spiritual food and drank the same spiritual drink; for they drank from the spiritual rock that accompanied them, and that rock was Christ.

We need to recognise that Messianic Judaism, in its present phase, is a new movement, and sometimes its infancy does show! No baby has ever been born mature. If we recognise that God is doing a new thing in our day, then we Messianic Jews also need to recognise the great debt we owe to those in the mainline churches, without whose vision and encouragement we might not, humanly speaking, now exist. That debt I shall acknowledge with gratitude and enlarge on in the chapter on the history of the Messianic movement.

If we Jews have rightful cause to point out the legacy of antisemitism that remains in the Church, then we Messianic Jews at least need also to express our gratitude for the support we receive in the Church, not only in our day, but also for the vision some Christians have had in past generations. They saw their vision, for a variety of reasons, like the seed in the parable of the sower, seeming to be choked or to become seriously dehydrated, in their own day. They would rejoice (indeed in heaven they are rejoicing) at what the Spirit of the Lord is doing in our time.

CHAPTER 2

Messianic Judaism: An Historical Perspective

W E ARE ALL AWARE, however dimly, that Christianity began as a faith within the Jewish community of Israel. Jesus was a Jew, the apostles were Jewish, so were the 3000 who came to faith in Jesus at the Jewish festival of Shavuot (Pentecost) and the 5000 who came to faith after the healing of the beggar at the Temple gate (Acts 4:4)

> Now there were staying in Jerusalem God-fearing Jews from every nation under heaven (Acts 2:5).

It was to these pilgrims that Peter the Jew addressed the Gospel as one Jew speaking to others.

> Then Peter stood up with the Eleven, raised his voice and addressed the crowd: 'Fellow Jews and all of you who live in Jerusalem, let me explain this to you; listen carefully to what I say.... Men of Israel, listen to this: Jesus of Nazareth was a man accredited by God to you by miracles, wonders and signs, which God did among you through him, as you yourselves know (Acts 2:14,22).

Not until we come to the conversion of Cornelius in Acts 10 do we find a non-Jew among the believers. From the middle of the 2nd century CE the Church became a predominantly Gentile organisation, but there was probably never a time when Jewish believers were not present among its membership.

After the New Testament period, most of the time, numbers were small, and as each person came to faith they were absorbed within the larger Christian community of Gentile origin.

Following on from the evangelical revival of the 18th century, the trickle has become a stream. Whilst it may be premature to say that the stream has become a torrent, it is clear that the Lord is doing a new thing (or at least something not experienced since the New Testament period) which has to do not just with the numbers of Jews coming to faith in Jesus as Messiah, but also with the way in which we Jews express our new-found faith.

THE KISHINEFF EXPERIENCE

In the middle of the 19th century Joseph Rabbinovitch, a Jewish teacher and lawyer from Kishineff, the capital city of Bessarabia, during a time of intense Russian persecution of his people, went to the Holy Land, having come to the conclusion that the only salvation for them would be their return to the land of their fathers, where they could have their own state and be at last once more secure and free. On his arrival he began to read the New Testament, which had been recommended to him for providing reliable descriptions of historic localities in the Holy Land. As he turned his eyes toward the reputed site of Jesus' crucifixion he remembered the saying of the prophet Isaiah

> Surely he took up our infirmities and carried our sorrows, yet we considered him stricken by God, smitten by him, and afflicted (Is 53:4).

As he thought about other New Testament Scriptures, it became increasingly clear to him that Jesus was the Messiah promised to his people. Rabbinovitch returned to Russia with a clear conviction that his new-found faith must be shared with his people, but in a thoroughly Jewish context. His preaching and writing became widely known in many parts of Russia, and in Bessarabia he founded 'The Community of Messianic Jews, the Sons of the New Covenant,' in Hebrew *Yehudim Meshichiim Bney Brit Hadashah*. Its founding was completely independent of Christian missionary activity and its influence was experienced as far as Austro-Hungary in the West and Siberia in the East.

Toward the end of the 19th century another Jewish believer, in a book called *The Christian Movement amongst the Jews of Kishineff* quoted Rabbinovitch.

My spiritual work was not influenced by a church or denomination, nor did it come about by human help, but only through the goodness and great mercy of God. He revealed to me that the synagogue and contemporary Judaism are unable to help our Jewish people and that the only means of salvation for us as a people and as individuals is believing in Jesus, the Messiah of whom the prophets had spoken, the Redeemer of the world. *This gave my endeavours a specific character, unlike the work of missionaries.* From the very outset it was my heart's desire to bring together people and the words of the Messiah, which are spirit and life, in order that they might, by the power of the Holy Spirit, recognise Jesus as Messiah and Son of the Living God.[1] (Italics mine.)

Despite much opposition from his own people, a large number of Jews came to faith in Jesus, not only in his home town but throughout that part of Russia and indeed throughout Eastern and Central Europe. The influence of the movement grew from strength to strength and on into the 20th century, and although its roots and identity were separate from the missionary activity of the Church, it was in no way separatist in its outlook. Eventually it met up with that missionary activity and each influenced the other, to the mutual benefit of both. The fruits of this rich ministry cannot be catalogued here in detail, but by way of example, the coming to faith in Romania of Richard Wurmbrand will suffice to place the vitality of this movement in the annals of Christian history. Were it not for the upheavals that shook Europe and Asia, leading up to the Second World War which so decimated the Jewish population and vitality of Europe, the movement in Kishineff would have been indisputably recognised as the forerunner of the Messianic Jewish revival of our times.

What makes this particularly relevant at this moment in history, as the focus of so much of our attention once again turns towards Russia and Eastern Europe, is the amazing number of Jews there whose faith is already in Messiah Jesus, and the general openness of other Jews to the message of new life through faith in him. When we can get a true perspective of history on this, it may well be that we shall look to Kishineff to find the wellspring of our theme. Those who wish to read up this fascinating movement in greater detail will find their interest amply rewarded in a series of articles by Rev Eric Gabe.[2]

As freedom to travel, and freedom of information has become more accessible in the ex-Eastern Block countries, so others are researching this vital part of church history, and the full scale of its importance is yet to be realised.

THE HEBREW CHRISTIAN ALLIANCE

With the renewal of biblical emphasis in the 18th-century evangelical revival, came the rise of missionary work and the realisation that the Gospel was 'first for the Jew' (Rom 1:16), which led to the founding of 'The Church's Ministry among the Jews'[3], and other similar societies, through which a good number of Jewish people found faith in Jesus. These people generally described themselves as 'Hebrew Christians' (ie Christians of Jewish origin).

From the 19th century, groups of such believers began to found Hebrew Christian Alliances (HCA) in various countries for the purpose of maintaining their cultural identity. The first such Alliance was the British Alliance, founded in 1866. Other national Alliances followed and in 1925 the International Hebrew Christian Alliance was created as an umbrella organisation. For the purpose of church membership, however, individual Jewish believers also joined one of the mainstream denominations, usually (as with most missionary work) the denomination through which they came to faith. In fact church membership was considered the first loyalty: HCA membership was for additional informal fellowship with others of like background and cultural identity.

What was different in Kishineff was that relatively large numbers of Jews within the same community came to faith without the involvement of external missionary activity. What came into being was an indigenous Jewish movement which described itself as 'Messianic Jewish' rather than 'Hebrew Christian'. Lest we are tempted to think that this is a mere playing with words, or perhaps the founding of yet one more denomination, my aim will be to show that this is an important and sovereign work of God in which he is not only grafting back some of the original branches but, more significantly, restoring the whole Church onto its Jewish roots.

THE CHURCH'S MINISTRY AMONG THE JEWS

About the same time that God was beginning to reveal Yeshua to the Jewish people in Russia, he was preparing a group of Christians in England to enter into this sphere of service. In 1809 the Church's Ministry among the Jews (as it is now called) was formed. Such was the scope and vision of its leaders, that a nine acre site was obtained and a complete Hebrew Christian community was established. A visitor from Germany, Dr C.G. Barth wrote,

> Amongst the immense number of the inhabitants of London, a few are acquainted with the miracle which is being performed in the midst of them. They scarcely know that, at one of the extremities of this vast city, there exists a place called Palestine Place, nor do they know what passes there…The place…seems like a small town…In the middle stands the church…and on each side are neat houses and their gardens…a Hebrew inscription on the front of the church informs you that it is consecrated to the Christian worship of Israel. The service is performed in Hebrew and English, and the psalms are there sung in their own sacred tongue as of old on Mount Moriah.[4]

The society prepared several translations of the New Testament into Hebrew, as well as the Book of Common Prayer, and if this seems like the old colonial style 'empire building' we need to realise that in its day it was quite revolutionary! Only God sees the end from the beginning. All of us are children of our age: how can we be otherwise?

Among the notable leaders of the society in those years, Lewis Way's contribution to the Jewish cause is particularly notable as it links directly with what God was doing in Russia. Way visited Russia and developed a deep relationship with the Czar, through whose auspices he was invited to present a long and detailed Protocol to the Crowned Heads of Europe at the Aix-La-Chapelle Congress in 1818, in which his first point called for civil and social rights for the Jewish People, without any disparity with Christians. Again, if this seems basic to us, we need to realise that it was a revolutionary request in its day. Certainly the beginning of the second part of his protocol, entitled 'The Moral and Political

Aspect' would be seen as far-reaching and visionary by any standards. Lewis Way addressed the political leaders of Europe, some of the most powerful men in the world thus:

> The final re-establishment of the Jews in their land is a fact based on the infallible authority of the word of God. It is clear that all measures opposing this gracious dispensation will clash with the views of Providence, and will lead nowhere.[5]

I was privileged to preach at the 175th anniversary service of Lewis Way, in what was the chapel he built at his home, Stansted Park, West Sussex, now the home of the Earl and Countess of Bessborough. To indicate something of what God was doing through him and others at this time, I quote from the introduction to the service.

> You might wonder what two eccentric ladies, a group of oak trees, a corkscrew, two chapels, two unrelated Ways and a vast fortune have to do with the history of CMJ.
>
> The story starts in 1811 when two ladies, Mary and Jane Parminter, built a small chapel at their home 'A La Ronde' near Exmouth, Devon. They called it 'The Point of View', their point in view being the bringing of Jews to faith in Jesus prior to their promised return to Palestine. Nearby they planted some oak trees, with the stipulation that they should not be cut down until this event took place.
>
> A few years earlier, a thrifty Christian land agent from London, called John Way, was looking for a suitable legatee. He invited a distant relative to supper, and when a bottle of port was produced the old man found difficulty in removing the cork. The young relative thereupon drew from his waistcoat pocket a corkscrew. This incident led the elder Way to decide that 'any man who goes about with a corkscrew in his pocket is not likely to make good use of wealth.' Accordingly, Thomas lost his fortune by the turn of a corkscrew.
>
> One day John Way happened to be walking in The Temple in London when he noticed a plaque with the name 'Lewis Way'. Eventually the two unrelated namesakes met, and this led to a close friendship. Lewis Way was a young barrister with a charming disposition. He possessed marked ability and had wide Christian interests. These attributes strongly appealed to the older man,

and in due course the younger became possessed of his fortune– £300,000 'to be used for the glory of God.'

While seeking the Lord's will for the use of this money, Lewis Way visited his wife's family in Devon and one afternoon he happened to ride past 'A La Ronde'. The story of the chapel and the oaks made a deep impression on him, and he felt the call of God to devote his time, energy and fortune to bringing the Jewish People to a knowledge of their Messiah and restoring them to the Land of Israel. He pursued this call with great zeal and effort for the rest of his life; he gave much of his wealth to the Society and was one of its early founders.

After becoming ordained in 1817 he made a remarkable journey to Russia to enlist the Czar's help in purchasing land in Palestine. At the Czar's suggestion Lewis presented a paper relating to the Jewish People to the European Congress at Aix-La-Chapelle in 1818.

Earlier Lewis Way had bought Stansted Park estate in Sussex. He renovated the chapel and designed a special stained glass window unique in being the only window in a Christian place of worship which is wholly Jewish in design and symbolism. In 1819, after the consecration service when the house was full of guests, Lewis was missing. His wife found him alone, kneeling before the altar, while by his side was a paper in which he had solemnly dedicated the Stansted estate to God to be used as a college for the training of Jewish and other Christian workers.

Many of Lewis Way's plans were not destined to mature in his day, but we can see today how God is fulfilling His promises for the Jewish People.

Oak trees still stand at 'A La Ronde' now owned by the National Trust. The Earl of Bessborough has recently opened Stansted Park to the public.

RESURGENCE OF LIFE

The movements that began through Joseph Rabbinovitch at Kishineff, and through men like Lewis Way in England, influencing a large part of Europe, appeared to meet an untimely death with the increasingly traumatic events of the Crimean and two world wars, leading to the decimation of the Jewish communities of Europe.

But death was followed by resurrection. In 1948 came the rebirth of the State of Israel, and in the 1960s the Holy Spirit began to move amongst the 'flower power' dropouts of the USA, many of whom were from Jewish communities. Again Jews who believed that Jesus was their Messiah formed communities with minimal contact with, or knowledge of, the mainline churches.

There was, however, one big difference. In Kishineff the Jews who came to faith in Jesus came from a deeply religious background, and they had both the theological and the pastoral resources to develop their own spirituality. In the American scene the newly born Messianic movement had neither, and the new believers were initially nurtured in the mainline denominations, especially in the Baptist Church. It was within this group that the organisation 'Jews for Jesus' was born. The name was not so much a 'job description', ie to win Jewish people for Jesus, as an 'identity description'; Jews who have come to believe that Jesus is the Messiah. However, partly because of the sense of community already binding the dropouts together, plus the relatively large numbers involved when compared with the numbers involved in previous generations, apart from the Kishineff experience and its outworking, and partly because the founding of independent congregations is much more part of the American scene than is the case in Europe, within a generation a vibrant independent Messianic movement spread through the USA. From there Messianic Congregations have come into being in practically every country where a Jewish community exists, not least in the land of Israel itself.

As we look at the origins of Messianic Judaism and its ambivalent relationships, sometimes even stormy relationships with Judaism and Christianity, we shall have to face the questions that are frequently asked: 'Just how Jewish is Messianic Judaism, and just how Christian is it?' Is it, as some would say, an unstable mishmash of two great world religions, each with an authentic and honourable life and history of its own? Or is it, as it sees itself, a genuine bridge with its piers firmly grounded in both communities?

At the risk of repeating what many potential readers already know, I shall describe these two communities anew. It is a very Jewish thing to repeat our story, even among people who know it well, because always there is a different context, a fresh perspective, which leads to new and sometimes radical reinterpretations.

A classic example of this is Stephen's speech to the elders of his nation in Acts 7. There was nothing in its content that the elders would not have known already, and there was little with which they would have disagreed. But Stephen's perspective was so different, his conclusions so radical, that nothing short of stoning, the punishment for blasphemy, could be countenanced. I hope that readers will be patient and not skip over those sections about their own faith that they feel they know already, and if they find the conclusions too radical I trust their response will be more gentle!

CHAPTER 3

Emerged from the Chrysalis

JUST OVER TWENTY YEARS AGO Michael Harper visited a neighbouring parish to speak about a new phenomenon that was being experienced in many churches, the baptism of the Holy Spirit.

I was excited by what I heard! For years, long before I had heard of this movement, it had seemed to me that those wonderful workings of God in the New Testament should be as available to us now as they were then. But whenever I queried this with people who I thought should know, they always managed to convince me with seemingly deep reasons, why this should not be so. Since I had not experienced these things myself, and since I did not know anyone else who had, there was nothing more that I could do. Increasingly, however, I felt that to say these gifts were for then, but not for now, was not far short of saying that they didn't really happen then. At the very least, if they happened only then, and not now, just what relevance did those Scriptures have for us?

That way of looking at the text may have been more acceptable in evangelical circles as not undermining the truth and authority of Scripture, but for all practical purposes there did not appear to be much difference. So when Michael spoke I was ready to hear and respond; eager and ready to receive all that the Holy Spirit wished to give me.

But there were surprises in store which took me back over thirty years and which have challenged and radically transformed my life and the direction of my ministry ever since. Ephesians 3:20 has proved abundantly true in my life.

> Now to him who is able to do immeasurably more than all we ask
> or imagine, according to his power that is at work within us...

31

God has indeed done more than I could possibly have imagined, and perhaps more than I would have asked for, had I known at the time where it would lead!

My preaching, teaching and personal prayer life took on a new relevance. Our church began to experience a new dynamism. There were those who would question what was happening, and a few who eventually left. These things I was ready for, but other things took me totally by surprise.

There were new songs which ministered wonderfully to me. Jeanne Harper has a wonderful ministry in this field, and so did the Fisherfolk whom I first met at the Nottingham International Charismatic Conference organised by the Fountain Trust. I immediately invited them to visit our parish of Christ Church Bayston Hill, where they ministered several times during the following years. Quite unexpectedly, it was the Jewishness of the music, and the emphasis on Israel that stirred up deep feelings within me.

Of course I knew in my head that I was Jewish; how could I ever forget? I had come to England with my brother in July 1939 from Czechoslovakia with the Kindertransport movement. My parents, and most of the rest of my family were not granted visas by the British government, and so had to stay behind and perish in Hitler's camps. I was seven years old when I came, but how could I ever forget?

We transportees all had a Jewish legal guardian, but were placed wherever the Jewish Refugee Committee could find a home for us. I was fostered by a lovely practising Christian family in Sheffield. No pressure was put on me, but quite naturally I joined their family life, especially as they had a son of their own, just a few months older than myself.

When the Refugee Committee realised what was happening they felt it necessary to counter the Christian influence on me, but not being able to justify actually removing me from this family, they sent me to a Jewish boarding school at Haslemere. It was a small coeducational school with about eighty pupils, and as I was still only about twelve years old, who was I to object? I certainly have happy memories of my three years there. I was in a Jewish environment in term time, and back with my Christian foster family in the holidays.

Just before my Bar Mitzvah I came to the very clear conclusion that what I had been taught about Jesus was true and therefore wrote to my guardian to request permission to be baptised. He made arrangements for me to see a rabbi in Sheffield to discuss the matter, and, to cut a long story short, I was baptised at St John's Church, Worksop, on November 10th 1947, our family having moved from Sheffield by that time. Needless to say, I was not welcome to return to the boarding school!

It was at this point that unknowingly I was sucked into a stream of two thousand years of church history, when both my new church and my foster parents strongly urged upon me that now I was no longer Jewish: I had now joined God's new Israel, the Church, and I should put my Jewishness behind me. Because of the climate in the church it probably did not occur to them to teach me anything different, and I was not equipped to question it. I never forgot that I was Jewish, but something within me 'died', though I cannot say that I was aware of what had happened.

The next fairly uneventful years led to an engineering degree at Nottingham University, two years in the Royal Air Force, a year in industry, and finally four years at the London College of Divinity at Northwood for ordination training. It was here that I first met with the Church's Ministry among the Jews and the Hebrew Christian Alliance. I became interested in them, but rather because of what I had been, not because of what I was.

Following marriage and ordination in 1961, my wife Elizabeth and I served in two parishes in the Manchester diocese, the second being in a very Jewish area, West Didsbury, where we had two synagogues in the parish, one Ashkenazi and the other Sephardi. To be truthful, this probably meant more to Elizabeth than to myself; she loved shopping at some of the kosher shops!

In 1966 I was appointed vicar of Christ Church Bayston Hill, where, a few years later, the events that were to transform my life began.

One of the new things in my life that the Lord was giving me was a counselling ministry. This did not come as a 'word from the Lord', but rather just in the way people began to respond to my pastoral care. I went on a residential counselling training course run by Dr Frank Lake on 'The Healing of the Memories', and by the middle of the second day of the conference I was no longer a student, but a client. My innate Jewishness burst through the barrier of suppressed memory into the vital centre of my being.

For the next months I went into an 'automatic pilot' kind of existence (though not nearly so consistent, reliable or predictable). I then went into what I can now describe as a tunnel experience. Entering as a very 'Gentilised' Christian, I came out as a Messianic Jew, though for years more I did not use that term simply because I had not heard it. I think I understood something of how Moses must have felt, waking up one morning, realising in his guts that he was not an Egyptian, but Jewish. In his confusion (unless I am simply transferring my feelings onto him) he went out and 'proved' his Jewishness by killing an Egyptian, and the Lord had to send him into the wilderness for forty years to teach him that there were better ways to be Jewish.

My reaction, and the Lord's discipline, were thankfully less dramatic, but none the less painful and bewildering. I had thought my past was well and truly in the past. My testimony had been that I had 'forgiven and forgotten'. Now that memories were not simply being restored to my mind, but to the centre of my being, I realised that I had not at all forgiven, but simply put my pain in a box, slammed the lid, locked the box and thrown the key away. Gently the Lord put the key back in my hand. By his grace, and with the support of Elizabeth and others in my parish who had the gifts, the grace and the courage to minister to their own 'minister', and with the tolerance and patience of my young family, who could not have known exactly what was happening, the box was opened and the past relived and healed.

How could I know that my healing was real? How could I know how long it was to last? What 'sign' would the Lord give that the butterfly had at last emerged from the chrysalis? There seemed no answer, but one day, I was listening to a tape by David Pawson in which he recounted a story told him by the American army chaplain to the Nazi leaders at the Nurnberg trials. Nearly all the top Nazi leaders, so the story goes, accepted Christ on the eve of their executions. My head told me that it was all humbug and hypocrisy, and in any case probably not true. But my heart sang with joy that these men had found forgiveness, peace and the way to eternal life. My heart refused to join the cynicism of my head, so my head had to join the joy of my heart! I had finally found the assurance that my healing was complete, or as complete as it can be this side of heaven.

For the next few years we were all running to keep up with what God was doing. Church membership quadrupled, and we built a new church centre. The Lord called us to a ministry of loving care for people with severe mental handicap and, in conjunction with Christian Care for the Mentally Handicapped, we built a life care home for ten residents in the grounds of the new church. The Lord blessed us abundantly, beyond our wildest dreams, and I came to realise that one of the main reasons was that here was a church that took Genesis 12:3 seriously. 'I will bless those who bless you...'. The church rejoiced with me in what the Lord was doing in the life of its Jewish vicar; they encouraged me not only to explore my roots, but to share my new life with them and to teach them about the Jewish roots of their own faith.

In the four years since we left that parish, its love for the Jewish People and its desire that they come into a real knowledge of Jesus as their Messiah has not abated. The church has continued to grow, and recently the buildings have been more than doubled in size. However Genesis 12:3 is not another version of an 'easy believerism' prosperity Gospel. The church has not grown without sacrifice and pain, but God is true to his word and has given us ample evidence of this.

God had given me a lovely wife and three wonderful children, and in the church he had given me a marvellous extended family. In the title of one of the traditional Jewish Passover songs 'Dayenu' (it would have been enough for us). It might have been enough for me, but seemingly it was not enough for God. Out of the blue, without any search or involvement on either of our parts, my brother and I were reunited with an uncle, our father's brother, who was living in Los Angeles, and with two cousins, the children of our father's sister, who were living in New Jersey. We had not seen one another for fifty years. Needless to say there were joyful reunions, as the remnant of our family was being pieced together.

In 1991 Elizabeth and I, together with my brother and his wife, felt that the time had come to go back to Czechoslovakia and

Germany, and search out our roots. That visit was amazing! In the little village of Vitkov, in Northern Czechoslovakia, very near to the Polish border, we found, and were invited into our family house where we had lived, together with our parents, maternal grandparents and great grandparents, in the years leading up to our coming to England. One of the most moving parts of the visit was to stand on the station platform where we had said our final goodbye to our parents, who had arranged our journey to England, knowing that it would be most unlikely that they would be able to follow.

We then drove to Dresden in Germany, where we had also lived until 1937, expecting to find the worst, knowing how badly that city had been devastated. However, in our part of the suburbs no damage had been inflicted, and it was a simple task to find the flat where we had lived. The whole area was just as we had left it, except that the newly planted saplings in the grounds of our block of flats had matured; and our flat now sported a Sky TV dish by the front window! Even our childhood sandpit was intact in the grounds. We had photographs with us dating back to the late 20s and early 30s to prove that our memories were not playing tricks!

Last year, at our children's suggestion, we returned to Czechoslovakia, because they also wanted to trace out something of their parents' roots, though we did not return to Dresden on that visit. During that visit I was able to obtain a copy of my birth certificate from the 'Matrica', the Registry of Births in Prague. (It proves that I am as old as I feared I was.)

On our way home we visited yet one more distant cousin, now living in Munich, who had lived in Vitkov, and who had spent the war years in England, though we did not know it; and neither did he about us. Again, the way we found one another without even seeking is one of those miracles of God's timing. We also were able to make contact with some Czech and German Church leaders, and return visits will now no doubt continue.

I said earlier that it was the *Jewishness* of the renewal movement that sparked so much of what was happening in me to life. It came therefore as something of a shock to discover that this music, much of which came from the worship being experienced in the House Church movement, was actually their way of saying to the historic denominational churches, 'You thought that you were the New Israel. But you are wrong: we are!' God was indeed using the renewal movement, both in the new House Church movement and within the historic denominations, to bring new life to the whole Church. Of that I have no doubt. But thank God that he does not have to wait until we have all our theology correct before he does so.

It seems clear to me that 'New Israel' or 'Replacement' theology is not true to biblical teaching. There is only one way of salvation for all people, Jew and Gentile, and that is through the atoning sacrifice of Jesus. In Jesus all believers, Gentile and Jewish, are one. These things are beyond dispute. But God's covenant with the physical children of Abraham, Isaac and Jacob has not been abrogated. It is from this 'olive tree' that unbelieving branches have, for the time being, been broken off and Gentile believing branches grafted in. But this is very different from the 'Replacement' teaching which has been the focal point of so much church teaching over its long history. If God does not continue faithful to the Jewish People, how can Gentiles be sure that he will remain faithful to them. Have they been any more faithful? And even if they have, does that not bring in the whole false doctrine of merit? If God is not faithful to the Jewish People, then there is nothing for Gentile believers to be grafted into.

It is this belief that has motivated my commitment to Messianic Judaism and has led to the writing of this book. May God guide both readers and writer as together we seek to follow Jesus in the way he went about his work.

CHAPTER 4

Our Covenant Keeping God

FOR YEARS I USED TO travel regularly to London for particular committee meetings, I arrived at Euston, descended into the underground system, and after two or three changes arrived at my destination. Sometimes, when I had time to spare, I surfaced at my interchange stations and got to know the immediate vicinity quite well, but I never put it all together. Then I went to live and work in London, got to know its geography more closely, and realised that when I looked at Euston and my destination in its context, I could have made the journey by bus, or even walked, in half the time.

We can be a bit like that with the Bible. We are well acquainted with some parts, perhaps even many parts, but somehow we never 'put it all together'. That's what we shall do now.

THE ABRAHAMIC COVENANT

We know the story of the Fall, the Flood and the Tower of Babel so well that I shall not repeat them here. But have we put them together and asked why they are there? If Adam and Eve, created in innocent perfection, fell into sin, wasn't it a bit naive of God to think that Noah could do any better? Noah was a righteous man, but then so had Adam been. Though Noah was described as righteous, he certainly didn't share Adam's initial sinless perfection. Did it surprise God that the history of sin, so to speak, repeated itself? Could it be that the Bible begins with these stories in order to nail once and for all any idea that humankind's best efforts and intentions can overcome evil inclinations?

Then God called Abraham. We notice something different here. Not what we are told about Abraham, but when we are *not* told about him. We don't know whether, like Noah, he was a 'righteous' man. Certainly as the story unfolds, his good qualities, as well as his weaknesses, become evident. But the important thing to notice is that this is not the basis of God's call. The important element is that God, in his sovereign purposes, chooses Abraham and enters into an unconditional covenant with him, irrespective of his moral and spiritual qualities.

> The LORD had said to Abram, 'Leave your country, your people and your father's household and go to the land I will show you. I will make you into a great nation and I will bless you; I will make your name great, and you will be a blessing. I will bless those who bless you, and whoever curses you I will curse; and all peoples on earth will be blessed through you' (Gen 12:1-3)

This covenant is developed in chapters 15 and 17 and renewed through Isaac and Jacob. Thus the blood line, now known as the Jewish People, came into being.

THE MOSAIC COVENANT

The 'Who is a Jew?' debate rumbles on in the Jewish community, especially in the State of Israel, where all Jews have the inborn right to make aliyah (return to the Land) and be granted Israeli citizenship. But now the numbers are so great, and sections within the Israeli religious establishment have a vested interest in preventing Messianic Jews from making their home in Israel. Their problem is that a purely racial definition, such as the biblical one, cannot exclude Messianic believers, while a rabbinic religious definition would exclude secular Jews, who make up the vast majority in the Land.

The biblical definition is clearly a racial one, though of course God expects Jews to live up to the high standards of the covenants he has graciously given to them. These standards were given to Moses through the Covenant of the Law, which is not, as is so often asserted (usually by Gentiles), the way by which Jews aim to attain righteousness; rather it is a kind of 'National Constitution'. 'As my Covenant People,' says God, 'this is how you are to live.'

These covenants are 'given', they are not negotiated, and from

Gods's side they are absolute, unconditional, irrevocable and unbreakable. There are different aspects to the covenants: Israel's obedience will bring blessing, disobediance will bring punishment and discipline. But these latter are also signs of God's faithfulness to his covenant, not, as is sometimes thought, his abrogation of them.

Israel at times may seem to break the covenant, Jacob (the schemer) may even try to 'renegotiate' the covenant.

> Then Jacob made a vow saying, '*If* God will be with me and will watch over me on this journey I am taking and will give me food to eat and clothes to wear so that I return safely to my father's house, *then* the LORD will be my God (Gen 28:20)

(implying if not... then he won't!).

But in fact the covenant will 'break' them, in the sense of bringing them under the hand of God's chastisement and discipline. As has been said, a man does not break the law of gravity by jumping off a tower. In fact the law of gravity breaks him!

THE 'ROYAL MARRIAGE' COVENANT

The covenant theme is next renewed with the Davidic Kingship Covenant of 2 Chronicles 13:5, which has Messianic connotations which we shall look at in more detail in a later chapter and the 'Royal Marriage' Covenant of Isaiah 62.

> For Zion's sake I will not keep silent, for Jerusalem's sake I will not remain quiet, till her righteousness shines out like the dawn, her salvation like a blazing torch. The nations will see your righteousness, and all kings your glory; you will be called by a new name that the mouth of the LORD will bestow. You will be a crown of splendour in the Lord's hand, a royal diadem in the hand of your God. No longer will they call you Deserted, or name your land Desolate. But you will be called Hephzibah, and your land Beulah; for the LORD will take delight in you, and your land will be married. As a young man marries a maiden, so will your sons marry you; as a bridegroom rejoices over his bride, so will your God rejoice over you (Is 62:1-5).

We need to understand this in relationship with Paul's teaching in Ephesians 5:25-33.

> Husbands, love your wives, just as Christ loved the church and gave himself up for her to make her holy, cleansing her by the washing with water through the word, and to present her to himself as a radiant church, without stain or wrinkle or any other blemish, but holy and blameless. In this same way, husbands ought to love their wives as their own bodies. He who loves his wife loves himself. After all, no-one ever hated his own body, but he feeds and cares for it, just as Christ does the church—for we are members of his body. 'For this reason a man will leave his father and mother and be united to his wife, and the two will become one flesh.' This is a profound mystery—but I am talking about Christ and the church. However, each one of you also must love his wife as he loves himself, and the wife must respect her husband.

The primary focus of this passage is usually taken to be marriage, using the church as an analogy, but verse 32 makes it clear that the primary focus is on Jesus and the Church, from which Christian marriage may derive a pattern.

How do we resolve the seeming problem of the two 'brides of God'; Israel and the Church? As we test the commonly held Christian assertion that the Church is the 'New Israel': that the Jewish People lost their place as the covenant people of God when they rejected Jesus, we will realise, to put it bluntly, that this is saying that God has, after all he promised, broken his covenant with Israel. He has divorced his 'brown-eyed brunette', because she displeased him, and taken to himself a gorgeous 'blue-eyed blonde'. If this is the case, let the Church beware lest she also displease him. Who will be number three?

If some readers find this kind of talk almost blasphemous, then we need to really ask ourselves quite seriously if some of our thinking about the Church and Israel has not bordered on denying the true nature of God's covenant with Israel? This is not to deny that the 'brown-eyed brunette' has sometimes played fast and loose with God and distanced herself from the true nature of that covenant. We have a God-given picture of this in the Book of Hosea.

Hosea's wife, Gomer, is constantly going of with other lovers, but Hosea, in his constant love and faithfulness wins her back to himself. He brings her back under his roof but does not, for a period of discipline restore to her the joys of married love,

> Then I told her, 'You are to live with me for many days; you must not be a prostitute or be intimate with any man, and I will live with you' (Hos 3:3)

('Live with you', see NIV footnote 'I will wait for you'.)

The interpretation is in the next verse:

> For the Israelites will live for many days without king or prince, without sacrifice or sacred stones, without ephod or idol. (Hos 3:4)

Discipline, for Israel, would involve separation from all that was idolatrous, but it would also mean a period of deprivation of her intimacy with her God. Both these pictures of Israel are true, from the human side the wayward wife, but in the love and grace of God, 'a crown of splendour in the Lord's hand, a royal diadem in the hand of your God' (Is 62:3).

The Olive Tree

In what sense can the Church also be understood to be in that marriage covenant with God if Israel has not been rejected? Paul gives us the clue in another picture of Israel and the Church in Romans 11. Here the symbol is not wedded bliss, but the olive tree. Israel is seen as the cultivated olive tree from which some branches have been broken off, because of unbelief and disobedience. Wild branches from a wild olive tree (Gentile Christians) are grafted into their place, but the tree itself, its trunk and roots, remain fully Jewish.

> If some of the branches have been broken off, and you, though a wild olive shoot, have been grafted in among the others and now share in the nourishing sap from the olive root, do not boast over those branches. If you do, consider this: You do not support the root, but the root supports you. You will say then, 'Branches were broken off so that I could be grafted in.' Granted. But they were broken off because of unbelief, and you stand by faith. Do not be

arrogant, but be afraid. For if God did not spare the natural branches, he will not spare you either. (Rom 11:17-21).

The Gentile Christian branches feed on the same grace of God as do the natural Jewish branches, but the nourishment does not come independently of the Jewish tree.

We can now tansfer the outworking of this analogy back to the picture of the bride. Thje bride of Paul's picture in Ephesians has not replaced the bride of Isaiah's picture, but neither are they identical. No analogy can be pressed too far, or it breaks down, but the teaching is the same; the Church is only the bride in so far as it is grafted into Israel.

Paul recognises the limitations of his pictorial imagination; a good gardener would pick holes in it (Rom 11:24). He is conveying a deep truth which is basically beyond words to tell. And what is true of Israel is also true of the Church. Both, in their human nature, are like Gomer: yet both, in the eyes of their wonderful Husband are beloved and glorious. The tragedy is that the Church, in its teaching, has so often applied the beautiful attributes to itself and the debased characteristics to the Jews. This is the basis of what has come to be known as the 'Teaching of Contempt' (for the Jews) which runs like a sore throughout much of Church history and continues to colour Jewish/Christian relations to this day.

The Fig-Tree

There is one further picture, from the Gospels, that relates to this theme which will naturally lead us into our next section.

> Then Jesus told this parable: 'A man had a fig-tree, planted in his vineyard, and he went to look for fruit on it, but did not find any. So he said to the man who took care of the vineyard, "For three years now I've been coming to look for fruit on this fig tree and haven't found any. Cut it down! Why should it use up the soil?" "Sir," the man replied, "leave it alone for one more year, and I'll dig around it and fertilise it. If it bears fruit next year, fine! If not, then cut it down"' (Lk 13:6-9).

We are not told the end of the story, which obviously relates to Jesus' own ministry among his people. Traditionally it has been assumed that, despite a year's respite, the tree was ultimately for the chop. The Jewish People failed. There was no room left for them on the soil. They were thrown out of the vineyard, and ultimately almost into oblivion, and for much of history the Church has been either a passive bystander or even an active accomplice.

All too easily we identify the parable of the fig tree of Luke 13 with the narrative of the cursing of the fig tree in Matthew 21 and Mark 11. However there are clear differences, perhaps most importantly in the contexts. The account in Luke relates the fig tree to the ordinary people, both Galileans and citizens of Jerusalem.

> Now there were some present at that time who told Jesus about the Galileans whose blood Pilate had mixed with their sacrifices (Lk 13:1)

> Or those eighteen who died when the tower in Siloam fell on them—do you think they were more guilty than all the others living in Jerusalem? (Lk 13:4).

Jesus is saying that these people were no worse than the ordinary people, and the ordinary people no better. God is looking for fruitful lives from all his people, and in his mercy they are to be given more space and time.

The accounts in Matthew and Mark are a continuation of the temple cleansing episode, and the religious leaders' response to Jesus action. The judgment on the fig tree is therefore a dramatised demonstration of the judgment on Israel's leadership. This differentiation between God's dealing with the ordinary people of Israel and his dealing with their national and religious leaders is vital for our understanding of the Bible as a whole. The people are frequently portrayed as 'sheep without a shepherd' (eg Ezek 34:7-10; Mt 9:36).

While it would be as wrong to see in the teaching of Jesus a blanket condemnation of the leadership without qualification, there is a marked difference in his attitude to leadership and people. Because Jesus is the Good Shepherd, where the other appointed shepherds have failed, and because he is the gardener in the parable of Luke 13, he is pleading for a time extension, a staying of the hand of God's judgment, just as he was later to pray, 'Father forgive them, for they do not know what they are doing.'

The frequently recurring story of the Church is one of blanket condemnation of the Jewish People which is totally at variance with Jesus' attitude of pastoral care and the patient loving working out of his purposes.

THE NEW COVENANT

The crunch point for our understanding of this theme comes in Jeremiah's teaching on the new covenant, and its relationship with the New Testament letter to Messianic Jews, which, after all, is what the Letter to the Hebrews really is.

'The time is coming,' declares the LORD, 'when I will make a new covenant with the house of Israel and with the house of Judah. It will not be like the covenant I made with their forefathers when I took them by the hand to lead them out of Egypt, because they broke my covenant, though I was a husband to them,' declares the LORD. 'This is the covenant I will make with the house of Israel afte that time,' declares the LORD. 'I will put my law in their minds and write it on their hearts. I will be their God, and they will be my people. No longer will a man teach his neighbour, or a man his brother, saying, 'Know the LORD,' because they will all know me, from the least of them, to the greatest,' declares the LORD. 'For I will forgive their wickedness and will remember their sins no more.' This is what the LORD says, he who appoints the sun to shine by day, who decrees the moon and stars to shine by night, who stirs up the sea so that its waves roar–the LORD Almighty is his name: 'Only if these decrees vanish from my sight,' declares the LORD 'will the descendants of Israel ever cease to be a nation before me.' This is what the LORD says: 'Only if the heavens above can be measured and the foundations of the earth below be searched out will I reject all the descendants of Israel because of all they have done,' declares the LORD (Jer 31:31-37).

All too frequently Christians have been guilty of what must be called sloppy exegesis, in assuming that God's promise of a *new* covenant implies a *new* people as its recipients, especially as our minds are attuned to hearing the words 'new covenant' in the context of participating in communion services in the now largely Gentile Church. Let us take a more detailed look at the context and the content of this new covenant.

The context is clearly that it is made with the same group of people as the previous covenants, 'the house of Israel and with the house of Judah'(v 31). The basis of the covenant is the same as previously, namely that it is given as an act of sovereign grace and choice, not dependent on merit or desert. Any such ideas are specifically refuted in verse 32, 'because they broke my covenant' and verse 37, 'only if... will I reject...'. The extent of the covenant is seen to be to the end of time, verse 36, 'Only if these decrees (sun, moon, stars, sea, waves) vanish...'.

The content of the covenant is the same as the previous Mosaic covenant, ie 'my law', but instead of being written externally 'on tablets of stone', it is to be written 'in the mind and on the heart'.

The question which biblical expositors have had to grapple with since the Letter to the Hebrews was first written, and with which Messianic Jews have particularly to grapple with, is how this links up with Hebrews chapter 8, where the writer, quoting Jeremiah 31:31-34, says specifically that the new covenant has made the first one 'obsolete'; and what is obsolete and ageing will soon disappear' (Heb 8:13).

The relationship between grace and law is one that has been deeply debated in the church over the centuries, sometimes leaning towards a very legalistic position, and sometimes toward a very libertinian one. In his letter to the Galatians Paul sees 'legalism' as a temptation to which Jewish Christians are particularly prone, and 'libertinism' as something more attractive to Gentile Christians. But church history has shown the pendulum to swing equally wide in both directions in the largely Gentile Church. Augustine tried to balance the two in his famous aphorism 'Love God and do as you like', which may be perfectly true, but open to much misunderstanding and abuse.

For us Messianic Jews, who see ourselves as fully part of the historic people with whom God made the covenants, and yet also fully recipients of liberty we have in the Messiah, this debate is of particular relevance, and we live with an equally wide diversity of interpretation among ourselves. There are Messianic congregations where the norm for members is strongly Torah observant, including Kashrut (food laws), sabbath observances etc, strictly observed. This would be supported by an appeal to the words of Jesus:

> I tell you the truth, until heaven and earth disappear, not the smallest letter, not the least stroke of a pen, will by any means disappear from the Law until everything is accomplished (Mt 5:18).

Others will begin with teaching based on Hebrews 7, where the emphasis is on the high priesthood of Jesus not being in the line of Levi, and Aaron, plus Hebrews 7:12.

> For when there is a change of the priesthood, there must also be a change of the law.

As is the case for all believers, Jew and Gentile, who are committed to belief in the final authority and consistency of Scripture, the principle of interpretation is that the more difficult passages have to be interpreted so as not to conflict with the plain meaning of the more straightforward passages. The fact remains that we do not always agree as to which is which.

Messianic Jews, whatever our differences in lifestyle may be, would wish to affirm the following principles:

1. Our salvation is based wholly on the atonement given through the death of Jesus, not on Torah observances.

2. Jewish identity is based on the Abrahamic covenant, not on the Mosaic, so any reasonable divergence of view regarding the place of the Mosaic covenant does not affect our identity as Jews.

3. The freedom we have through Jesus from the bondage of the law gives us the liberty to choose to observe the law, should we so decide, as part of our identity as Jewish people. This is a freedom we need to respect among ourselves, and also a freedom we would ask our Gentile Christian brothers and sisters to respect.

The importance of a right understanding of the irrevocable nature of God's covenant with the Jews is not in any way to exalt Jewishness or Israel. Far from it, we would plead guilty to our own Scriptures' assessment of us as a stiff-necked people. We would stress, however, that a right understanding of the nature of the covenant is vital for our understanding of the nature of God. If it is possible that God could change his mind about his covenant with the Jewish People and Israel, then no Christian can be secure about God's faithfulness to his promise about salvation through faith in Jesus.

God's faithfulness to the Jewish People and the Christian doctrine of assurance of salvation hang on the same line, that God cannot lie, and that he means what he says and he says what he means. In the words of the song about love and marriage, and the horse and carriage, 'You can't have one without the other'.

CHAPTER 5

Am I Going for It or Not?
David

O N 23RD DECEMBER 1985 I committed my life to Yeshua.
I was walking around the park near where I work as I
had done hundreds of times over the years. I remember
sitting on a seat and saying 'Look I know it's true. Am I going for
it or not?' It was as simple as that. And there were some amazing
events that occurred immediately after I made the commitment
on that date.

I was born in London, in Swiss Cottage, in 1956. My mother
and my father are Orthodox Jews and always professed to follow
Judaism, so I grew up in a household where Judaism was pro-
moted but not always practised. I went to Hebrew classes, as all
Jewish boys did, I became 'Bar Mitzvah', and even before that I
was reading the Haftorah in the synagogue when I was about
seven. Both my father and grandfather were very keen for me to
do this, but the problem was that they wanted me to be that way,
but weren't that way themselves, so it left me with a bad taste.

I was a very firm believer in God up to the age of ten. I
couldn't understand why some people didn't believe. It all
changed in 1967; for some reason I remember very clearly the
Aberfan disaster. I was about eleven, and I couldn't reconcile
what happened at Aberfan with God. After that my relationship
with God really fell away and I was no longer interested. I went
through my Bar Mitzvah but after that fell away totally, which is
partly why my time at a Hasmonean Jewish School was pretty
boring; I didn't really learn much of what they were trying to
teach me because it seemed hypocritical and wrong. This is how I
progressed through my teens, being quite agnostic and even
antagonistic. I did my own thing. I went through a typical
teenage rebellion.

I worked in my family business for about 13 years. The environment was of a family who thought it important to keep up the Jewish traditions but seemingly without any real meaning to it; just for the sake of tradition. I had one particular uncle with whom I worked who was very orthodox, but he never really knew why; he just was. Working with these people was difficult, and I found that after about 6 or 7 years I started to question the ethics of my family and how they were living their religion, because they were always talking about it but never actually doing it.

One particular uncle fasted on all the fast days and did everything right. One day we were having lunch in the showroom and my uncle abstained from lunch. My father asked him, 'Why aren't you eating lunch?', and my uncle replied, 'It's the fast of Tammuz', as if everyone should have known, and we shouldn't have been eating lunch either. Dad looked at him and asked what the fast of Tammuz was, but my uncle could not answer. He didn't know what it was either; he didn't know why he was fasting, but he knew that it was a tradition, so he did it.

As the years have gone by, I have told that story a few times as it had quite an effect on me. It showed me that my family did things, but they didn't know why they were doing them, and I have found this to be fairly common among the Jewish people I know. From that point on I started to question more.

A lady in our work place, a coloured lady, was an avid Bible reader. She always asked questions to try and comprehend the ethics of my family. She and I would talk together a lot; she used to mention Jesus, 'Jesus said this and this'. I used to argue with her a little, not trying to disprove her, but just to understand her. Eventually I thought I saw some sense and meaning in what she was saying. In late 1984 and early 1985 I started to pick up and read books, and to look into the Bible for myself. That was the turning point for me.

My past experience made me mistrust people to such an extent that there was no way I would have listened to any evangelist, or anyone else trying to tell me about religion, because my family had been trying to do that for years, and they never practised what they preached. I had to prove to myself something was true before I could believe in it.

I started reading the New Testament in Matthew, and after

the first few chapters I started to understand Jesus' response to some of the Jewish leaders of the time. When he called them hypocrites he was actually saying what I was feeling. I had an instant link with Jesus, an instant agreement, if you like, with where he was coming from. From that point on I don't think it was ever a case of proving Jesus was the Messiah, I knew he was, but I suppose I just wanted more information, and so I delved further into the New Testament and back into the Old, and tried to understand the Scriptures. My way to the Lord came through my own reading of the Bible and books written by people who believed in him.

I identified with Jesus. I also got the feeling of his own Jewishness. What I felt was that Jesus had the real meaning of what Judaism was about. Jesus brought fresh insight into what a relationship with God could be.

I never felt that if Jesus was right and I wanted to follow him, I would have to stop being Jewish and become a Christian. On the contrary I believed that what Jesus professed was pure Judaism. I knew little about Christianity at this time. I had great difficulty with the name Jesus for quite some time because of all that had built up in my upbringing. There was never any sense that I was going after another religion. It was always something that appeared to be Jewish to me. At this time I did not know that there were other Jewish people who also believed in Jesus as Messiah.

Ruth, my wife, was pregnant at the time I made my commitment to Yeshua, and our daughter, Miriam, arrived on 6th February, just a few weeks later. In between time I left my job with the family business; I had been there for thirteen years. I can't imagine how I ever got the strength to walk out of the business because I knew nothing else. I didn't have a job to go to. It was just that God was with me and gave me the strength to do it.

I was going to sign on the dole, but in the meantime I made fur samples for the company with which I am now working. My father-in-law had said that if I made some samples, they could try and sell them. God's timing was perfect, as ever. I was at the factory getting some samples made when I got a phone call from Ruth saying that another firm had agreed to give me a trial for three months. I saw that as God saying to me, 'Look I don't want you on the dole. I've got other things planned for you'.

I joined the other firm a week before Miriam was born. The six weeks between making the commitment and Miriam being born was incredible. God was absolutely amazing. He just changed my whole life in that time, and I've never looked back since that day.

My new found faith put a strain on our marriage relationship. We had been married for seven years before I made the commitment. For a year and a half leading up to my commitment I had my head buried in books. I had been reading everything that even touched on religion, Hinduism, Buddhism, Islam, although not in any great depth. But all with a view to how this related to Jesus. Any Jewish person who makes a commitment to Jesus and whose partner doesn't, could go through quite a rough process.

Much of my time was spent in a book or going to church. Before my commitment I was going to All Souls', Langham Place, where I attended a group called 'Agnostics Anonymous'. They were wonderfully helpful. I would go with sheets of questions on every subject and I got a lot of questions answered. Through them I got to hear about, and then visited, the London Messianic Congregation. It was quite small at the time with about twelve or fourteen people. I continued to go to All Souls' for quite some time, but gradually I felt that I didn't want to lose the Jewishness that I had. I felt and still feel, that Jesus was Jewish, that he followed the Jewish ways, and it was something I wanted to do as well. I didn't want to lose my heritage and I wanted to follow our traditions, but with the added and new meaning that Jesus brought to them. So I joined the London Messianic Congregation. After a couple of years I left, because I didn't feel that it was altogether meeting my needs.

I joined the South Bank Fellowship in Richmond where I received very good basic teaching. Looking back, the Messianic Congregation was for more mature believers than I was at the time, and I think that it does no harm for Jewish people to go into the churches initially to understand Christianity and Christians. We are all brothers and sisters and it's good to see people express the same faith in a different way.

But the Church's way wasn't for me, and eventually circumstances led me to come back to the Messianic group, where I got involved in the music. I had played the guitar a lot in my early teens, but didn't pick it up again until I became a believer. Ever since then I have played the guitar regularly and have always been encouraged in that. In my present Messianic Congregation I find I can express my Jewishness through the Messianic music that we sing and play; it's a good way for me to express what I feel. It is different from belonging to a mainline church. We come from a different perspective but we reach the same point, which is Jesus. I see Messianic Judaism as bringing a true Judaism back to the Jews and also a true Christianity to the church.

My whole family know of my beliefs, apart from my grandfather who is 95 and has always been a very orthodox Jew. My mother asked specifically that I wouldn't say anything to him because it would upset him too much, so I haven't and I feel that is the right decision. My family accept me for what I am. My father is not very happy about it, but never discusses it. I think he thinks I'm being stupid, and that I will come back to the fold one day. The uncle with whom I used to work doesn't approve at all, and seems to imply that Jesus can't be the Messiah, because when he was at school he kept being bullied by Christian people saying that he killed Jesus. So he uses this as an excuse. The rest of my family, whom I am close to, come mainly from my wife's side, and all accept me for what I am and what I believe. We don't discuss it very much and I don't push it. If they want to know, they'll ask.

Ruth's early background was a little different from mine. Her father was brought up in an orthodox way, but her mother was very secular with not much interest, except in following some of the traditions which she picked out. For example, when they first got married they wouldn't have dreamed of having bacon in the house, but now it's not a problem if they want to have it. So Ruth was brought up in a typically secular Jewish household. They are openly secular and happy about it.

My hope for Messianic Judaism in North-West London is to see a community of believers who really do love each other, who are close to each other, who are able to worship together in freedom, in full knowledge of who Yeshua is, and who can celebrate his Messiahship. If that can happen in one group, it could spread quickly like fire. I think we are going through a process at the moment, when God is refining each of us and the time will come when it will happen. That's my vision in the short-term. In the long-term, my vision is to see my Jewish People accept Jesus for who he is.

CHAPTER 6

A Messianic Jewish Perspective on the Book of Acts

WHY DOES IT SO SELDOM dawn upon Christians that the Church has come into existence, not because of Jewish failure but out of Jewish faithfulness! So often the death of Jesus is seen as marking the end of the Jewish story. The race (to pick a metaphor) goes on, but the baton is now in the hands, not only of another team member, but of a different team. But God reverses their disobedience on Easter Sunday and on the Day of Pentecost. By looking at the book of Acts, with a Jewish believer in Jesus as our guide, we shall realise just how Jewish this book really is. God has not, after all, changed his team.

PENTECOST

Luke describes the coming of the day of Pentecost in a very Jewish way. So Jewish that in fact most translations miss the point. 'When the day of Pentecost came...' So, prosaically, most translations begin, totally missing the Jewish flavour of Luke's Greek. The King James translation gets it right, but whether it does so out of knowledge, or whether it is blindly seeking to be literalistic in its translation, we cannot tell. Luke tells us not just that the day of Pentecost had come, but that it had fully come.

In Judaism the fifty days between Passover and Pentecost are called the Waiting Days. The days are counted off (there is a term 'counting the omer') rather as Christians might count off the days of Advent. Passover is not complete without Pentecost, Pentecost is meaningless without Passover; the two belong indivisibly together. By using this complex Greek word *sunpleerousthai* (literally 'fully come together'), Luke is putting his book in a Jewish context, and if we miss that we shall misunderstand much of the teaching of the book. Of course we also know that in Christian terms Easter is completed in Pentecost, and Pentecost is meaningless without Easter, but that is precisely because they have grown out of, and complete, their Old Testament prototypes.

In Peter's sermon on the day of Pentecost we observe that he is addressing 'fellow Jews' (2:14), 'men of Israel' (2:22), letting 'all Israel' know (2:36). The three thousand who came to faith on that day were all deeply religious Jews from every corner of the Diaspora. Why else would they have come to Jerusalem, but in order to fulfil the law.

> Three times a year all your men must appear before the LORD your God at the place he will choose: at the Feast of Unleavened Bread, the Feast of Weeks and the Feast of Tabernacles (Deut 16:16).

The five thousand who came to faith just a little later (Acts 4:4); those followers of the Lord whose lifestyle has inspired so much of the developing patterns of Church life in our lifetime (Acts 4:32-35); those ordinary but Spirit-filled believers who, in a time of persecution fled Jerusalem but spread the Gospel as they went; Stephen the first martyr for the Lord; Peter, who challenged, and was willing to question the traditions of his people and go into a house of a Gentile in order to share Jesus; Paul the Pharisee, who became God's tireless and fearless messenger to the Gentiles, and who rejoiced in this ministry; these were all Jews and maintained their Jewishness to their dying day! Paul's testimony regarding Ananias confirms this, when he speaks of him as 'a devout observer of the law and highly respected by all the Jews living there.' (Acts 22:12).

Not until the conversion of Cornelius do we have any indication that there was a Gentile among the congregations of the believers. And what a ruffling of the feathers that caused! Peter was recalled to Jerusalem for an explanation. To their credit, these normally tradition-bound Jews discern God doing a new thing. He is at work, not in isolation from, but in continuation with these men and women of God's Abrahamic Covenant People. What might have been an exception for one God-fearing Centurion became the foretaste of further such ministry (Acts 11:19,20; 13:46,47.) This was too much for some of the more rigorous of the Jewish believers, who insisted that these new Gentile believers must become Jews if they are to be accepted into the Messianic Community of Jesus. (Acts 15:1).

> Some men came down from Judea to Antioch and were teaching the brothers: 'Unless you are circumcised, according to the custom taught by Moses, you cannot be saved.' This brought Paul and Barnabas into sharp dispute and debate with them. So Paul and Barnabas were appointed, along with some other believers, to go up to Jerusalem to see the apostles and elders about this question (Acts 15:1).

THE COUNCIL OF JERUSALEM

We all know (or think we know) the outcome of the Jerusalem Council, that the last vestiges of the old Jewish legalism were removed from the Church which then entered into the freedom of the Spirit, that freedom we all enjoy now. But that is not what was decided. It was agreed that those *Gentiles* who were turning to God should not be brought under the Law of Moses. There was absolutely no suggestion that Jewish followers of Jesus should abandon Torah observance, or that for Jews Torah observance was in any way incompatible with living in the freedom of the Spirit. In fact just the opposite was the case.

As Paul and Silas were sent on tour to tell the churches of the outcome of the Jerusalem Council, they came across a lovely believer, Timothy, the son of a mixed marriage. According to Rabbinic law, Timothy, the son of a Jewish mother, was Jewish, but probably because of the strength of the local culture, and through the influence of his Gentile father, Timothy had not been circumcised. So Paul circumcised him.

We will, no doubt, have heard sermons on Paul's weakening and bowing to Jewish pressure. Yet in Galatians 2:3 we find Paul standing up to fierce pressure in order to prevent the circumcision of Titus. We will have heard (and may have preached) sermons on Paul's wavering inconsistency, but two things stand out when this book is clearly seen in its Jewish context. First, if Paul had weakened to Jewish pressure in circumcising Timothy he would have lost all credibility as the apostolic agent of the Council of Jerusalem. Secondly, if we see the reasons behind Paul's decision to circumcise Timothy (Timothy was Jewish) and stand out so firmly against the pressure for Titus' circumcision, (Titus was a Gentile) we shall see that Paul was acting both courageously and in total consistency with the principles decided by the Jerusalem Council.

FIRST TO THE SYNAGOGUE

After Paul had completed his apostolic commission he reported back to the leaders of the Jerusalem Church whose ultimate oversight he obviously recognised. But on his way another event took place, the significance of which is frequently overlooked precisely because readers are not viewing events through Jewish eyes. Whilst Paul was waiting in Athens (Acts 17:16) he was greatly distressed to see the wholesale idolatry of that great city. We recall that his evangelistic instincts and his God-given commission as Apostle to the Gentiles lead him straight to the 'Hyde Park Corner' of Athens, the Areopagus. 'And the rest' as they say, 'is history'. In fact this somewhat truncated version of events misses out one vital move. Let's look at the text in detail.

> While Paul was waiting for them in Athens, he was greatly distressed to see that the city was full of idols. So he reasoned in the synagogue with the Jews and the God-fearing Greeks... (Acts 17:16f).

Not only is the fact of Paul's visit to the synagogue prior to his going to the Areopagus usually glossed over, so is that statement of purpose 'so'. Luke is clearly and intentionally telling us that because Paul was distressed by the idolatry of Athens he preached Jesus first in the Synagogue, where there wouldn't be an idol in sight. The whole episode would be meaningless unless Paul had a very clearly thought out strategy, 'First to the Jew' (Rom 1:16). It becomes clear that he believed the only way, or better, the correct way, the God-given way, to plant a congregation among the sophisticated pagans of Athens, was first to plant a congregation among its Jewish inhabitants.

This was not an isolated event. Wherever Paul went in his primarily Gentile ministry, his pattern was first to go to the synagogue. Five times in this book Paul states the priority of

Jewish ministry (13:46, 18:1, 22:21, 26:23, 28:20-28), and even after experiences of Jewish rejection, when he says 'from now on I go to the Gentiles', that is only for that situation. After he has moved on, he again goes first to the synagogue. So consistent is he that we can safely surmise that he is expressing what he believed to be a priority in the purposes of God.

This is not, as some might think, a kind of divine 'favouritism', a charge that has often been made when this kind of position is expressed. The full reasons behind it must ultimately rest in the mystery of God, but we shall begin to consider them later, as Scripture gives us some clear indications.

We return to Paul's reporting to the Jerusalem elders in Acts 21:17. The well-known passage arising out of this is frequently interpreted as a kind of sop to the more extreme of the Jewish followers of Jesus, but let us look at the passage objectively and in some detail.

After rejoicing at the conversion of Gentiles, James gives us a description of the Jerusalem Church: 'many thousands of Jews...zealous for the law' (v 20). This is presented as cold fact, there is no implied criticism of legalism, so often levelled unjustifiably against the Jerusalem believers. There then follows some misinformation... 'they have been informed that you teach all the Jews...not to live according to our (Jewish) customs...then everybody will know that *there is no truth* in these reports about you, but that you yourself are living in obedience to the law.' (vs 21-24).

We need to recognise both Paul's and the Jerusalem elders' total commitment to the working out of the Jerusalem Council's decision, and they both functioned fully within its guidelines.

As we move into the events following the misunderstanding of verses 27f, we come to the point where Paul spoke to the Jewish crowd in Hebrew and, in fact, got a good hearing until he spoke of his call to his Gentile ministry, which sparked such a violent reaction, 'Rid the earth of him! He's not fit to live!'

Several crucial points arise from this section. The first is that in spite of the tense situation, Paul got a good hearing for his testimony until that last point. This, together with the existence of such a large and vibrant Torah observant Jewish Church in

Jerusalem, clearly shows that things had moved on a lot since Peter and the other apostles had been given a summary trial and flogging for their public witness in Acts 3 and 4.

There clearly must have been some kind of accommodation between the Jewish leadership on the one hand, and James and the Church's leadership on the other, for such an enormous Jewish congregation of followers to exist so openly in Jerusalem, and for Paul to have been given such a quiet hearing.

In this climate Paul and the Church leaders could have made one of two choices, either of which would have made life far easier for them. The first would have been for the Jerusalem leaders to try and keep the new faith totally within its original context as a sect within Judaism. Paul's experience of the Jewish crowd's silent attention shows this could have been a real possibility. Paul's testimony regarding Ananias confirms this view.

Alternatively Paul, as the Apostle to the Gentiles, could have taken the faith of Jesus right outside its original context and declared it to be a totally new religion, born within Judaism admittedly, but now totally separate from it. Neither of these 'soft options' was taken. The hard decision was made that salvation through Jesus was for both Jew and Gentile (Rom 1:16); that the dividing wall of hostility had been broken down (Eph 2:14,15); in Christ Jew and Gentile become one (Gal 3:28). Yet just as male and female are one in Christ, equal but complementary, rather than identical, so with Jewish and Gentile believers. All too often the true nature of our unity in Christ has been lost at the cost of the biblical emphasis on the distinctiveness of each in the purposes of God.

CHAPTER 7

I have not felt converted.
Alison

M Y RELATIVES CAME ORIGINALLY from Romania, Russia and Poland. My family could not, by any stretch of the imagination, be considered close and in fact my brother and I fought like cat and dog. We were members of a reform synagogue and attended on a semi-regular basis until my brother's Bar Mitzvah, after which our attendance took the characteristics of uncomfortable 'high days and holy days' guilt.

I was born in the mid sixties and until the age of 10 I attended cheder (Hebrew classes), where I could never understand why we learned how to read Hebrew without understanding; nor why, in synagogue, people recited prayers in English and Hebrew which they didn't understand. I found the ritualistic stand-up/sit-down routine (liberally interspersed with recitations and songs) meaningless and empty. Yom Kippur struck me as the most meaningless of all the Holy Days—even this special day of fasting and opportunity to be near to God became a challenge point. 'Are you going to fast?' 'How long did you fast for?' Another important fact which struck me was that we had to wear our Sunday Best (if you'll pardon the expression!). This was always an embarrassment to me as I never felt my wardrobe was adequate enough. I would regularly wonder if God really cared what I wore—wasn't it more important how I felt?

At this point in time I believed in God, that I could personally pray, and that, if I was a 'good girl', some of my prayers would be answered. I believed that something terrible would happen to me if I read the New Testament or looked at a cross or crucifix. The names Jesus and Christ were somehow offensive to me.

In my early teens I went to a Jewish youth club which I enjoyed very much. As I grew older and was allowed to spread my wings, I became horrified by the Saturday nights spent hanging around Golders Green or Edgware station, with nothing to do other than to try to get a boyfriend, and make a lot of noise. At the age of 16 I left the Jewish scene and started experimenting with sex, soft drugs and got myself (to the mortification of my parents) an Irish Catholic boyfriend. I moved on the educational conveyor belt from O Levels to A Levels then straight onto higher education. At college, where there is a strong emphasis on parties, I was swept along with the social scene, and my Jewish identity slipped further away.

The next part of this explanation of my faith is best described in two parts, 'personal searching' and 'absorbing'.

My personal searching took place mostly at college. In my first year I had lengthy discussions on religion with a couple of friends who regularly attended the college Christian Society. I couldn't understand their faith which appeared to bring joy and purpose in their lives, but these discussions challenged my faith.

I took out books from the college library on different religions and cults; Hinduism, Islam, Buddhism, witchcraft, Judaism and Christianity. This investigation lead me into complete atheism. I no longer believed in God and all supernatural events were explainable through science or the power of the mind.

That summer I visited Israel for the first time. On disembarking the aircraft, being hit by the humidity of Ben Gurion airport, and setting foot in the Holy Land, I had a strong desire (which, in true British fashion, I curbed) to do the Pope thing and kiss the tarmac.

I had been told what a spiritual place the Wailing Wall was, but when I visited it I was completely uninspired. I have memories of an old cold wall with little bits of paper (written prayers) sticking out.

I returned to Israel the following summer, after a disastrous affair, to lick my wounds and repair my broken heart. I visited the Wailing Wall for a second time and had what can only be described as a spiritual experience. For the first time in my life I was overwhelmed with the knowledge that I was in the presence of God.

As regards 'absorbing', I was studying music at college and was inevitably exposed to a great deal of church/religious music.

This was through the various choirs that I sang with (regular Sunday Services at the local Anglican church, special services for eucharist, Easter and Christmas in the college chapel and the town's cathedral or in concerts with the college choral society). During all these occasions I didn't pay much attention to the meaning of the words other than at the conductor's direction.

During all religious events, when I was subjected to a sermon I would invariably try to while away the 'vicar-speak' by day dreaming, reading the prayer book forwards and backwards, or reading a novel. On a few occasions however I listened to what the preacher had to say. One sermon stuck in my mind regarding legalism, that is following rules because you feel you have to, or through fear, rather than willingly doing things for the love of God.

'What is important', he said, 'is not what you put into your mouth, it's what comes out.' As a Jew this made me sit up and listen. I couldn't understand why God wanted His people to keep such difficult food rules. However kosher you are there is bound to be someone who goes that one step further. Not eating pig products and shell fish, not having those products in the house, keeping meat and milk separate, using different cutlery and crockery, using different cooking utensils, having separate fridges, freezers and cookers, not eating foods that contain certain E numbers, the list is endless. To my mind, as long as the food was clean I would eat it, and if I ended up with some nasty food poisoning then it wasn't clean.

In addition, as a migraine sufferer I have to avoid certain trigger foods. With this in mind I was now being challenged by a man in a long black skirt and a dog collar that perhaps God's interest in my mouth was more centred on my tongue, which at times could be quite vicious, rather than keeping a long list of rules which are rabbinic additions.

The term following my spiritual experience in Israel we briefly studied the opera 'Salome' at college. This is the New Testament story of Salome's erotic dance for her lustful stepfather Herod (who was also her uncle), in return for John the Baptist's head on a silver salver. Being a babe of the Old rather than New Testament, I didn't know the details of the story, which are obviously quite important when studying a piece. The lecturer was in a hurry that day and didn't want to be bothered with telling me the story (and boring my fellow students), so she rather brusquely told me to read the story in the Gospels, which, I was to discover, are the first four books of the New Testament.

I spent the next few weeks trying to lay my hands on a Bible. This, to my surprise, was amazingly difficult. I found it ironic that fervently evangelistic door knockers are incredibly difficult to get off your doorstep when you'd rather be watching the latest soap on TV, but when you actually want a Bible you can't get one. I was eventually lent one by a friend and apprehensively started thumbing through that part of the Bible of which I had previously been scared.

I found out what I needed for college regarding the Salome story, but was fascinated by other the events, parables and lessons that were described. One particular passage that springs to mind is the parable in Luke 18:9-14. This describes two people praying in the temple. One is a religious man who rattles off a list of how wonderful he is, with an unhealthy pride in his piety, while the other is a man who is clearly ashamed of himself and is asking God's forgiveness. The message is, which one will receive the kingdom of heaven? The one who thinks his salvation is based on his good deeds, or the one who truly repents of his sins, prays for God's forgiveness and help in not repeating the sins?

Upon reading this I knew that Jesus was the Messiah that my people had been waiting for.

A Christian friend invited me to her baptism (baptism I was later to discover has strong links with the mikvah). I enjoyed the service but still didn't feel comfortable with the name Jesus. A few weeks later I asked the same friend I if I could accompany her to her church one Sunday. I think the colloquial expression is that 'she nearly fell off her perch'. At that service, the first that I had willingly chosen to go to, I met with God in a new way through praise, prayer and worship. Following the service, nibbling a non-kosher burger in a fast food restaurant, my friend asked me,

'Well then, what does it feel like to be a Christian?'

'I'm not,' I replied.

The conversation then went as follows

'Do you believe that Jesus existed?'

'Yes.'

'Do you believe he is alive today?'

'Yes.'

'Do you believe he is your personal Saviour and Messiah?'

'Yes.'

Well then, you're a Christian.'

'Yes, I suppose I am.'

The reason I've mentioned this is that even now I feel uncomfortable saying the words Jesus and Christ (and then of course Christian). To Gentile believers in Jesus who call themselves Christian, I am also a Christian. However, the names Jesus and Christ have Greek origins which to Jews convey feelings of persecution and hatred. I prefer the names Yeshua and Messiah, after all, he was Jewish wasn't he?

I spent several years attending an evangelical church where I felt more or less at home. The lack of understanding for my Jewishness, and the obvious Jewishness of Yeshua and most of his disciples was upsetting, but this was something I chose to ignore.

For various reasons I left that church in search of a congregation where I could gain a fuller (more Jewish) understanding of the Bible. I am now a regular attendee of a small Messianic congregation. Here I am not forced to ignore my background, rather I am encouraged to fulfil it.

This idea can be expanded across the 'conversion' argument. I have not at any time felt 'converted'. On the basis that the Messiah came first for the Jews I can only feel a fulfilment.

Although I can now see a sense of purpose in the Jewish religion, I have, at times, found everything very hard. Coming to terms with aspects of my life which I would rather forget, and standing up for faith in a Messiah which, in a technological world appears unnecessary to my people, is viewed with anything from indifference to contempt, and to my friends is seen as either compassion or weakness. My close relatives are in the 'know' but they think it is a passing phase. I wouldn't dream of telling other relatives for fear of causing embarrassment to my parents. I am saddened to think that, to the Jewish community in this country, it would probably be easier 'coming out' as a lesbian than as a Messianic Jew.

CHAPTER 8

God's Gifts are Irrevocable.
Israel in Paul's Letter to the Romans

IN WORKING ON THE THEME of God's purposes for the
Jewish People, we have to consider carefully Paul's letter to
the Romans. In many commentaries that have been written,
there is a wide diversity of views and interpretations expressed,
even among evangelicals, as regards the place of the Jewish
People in the purposes of God.

This is not the time or place to add yet one more commentary.
My aim is to highlight the issues as Paul raises them, and to point
to directions which will help towards clarifying a consistent train
of thought through the letter.

To highlight the problem we shall give quotations from three
respected evangelical commentators of different periods.

1. H.C.G. Moule, a previous Professor of Divinity at
Cambridge, and Bishop of Durham, in his commentary on
Romans (1894), but recently reprinted (1992), writes on 'all Israel
will be saved' (Rom 11:26):

> It has been held by some interpreters that this points to the Israel
> of God, the spiritual sons of Abraham.... But surely it does
> violence to words, and thought, to explain 'Israel' in this whole
> passage mystically. Interpretation becomes an arbitrary work if
> we may suddenly do so here, where the contrast between Israel
> and the Gentiles is the very theme of the passage. No; here we have
> the nation,...chosen with a choice never cancelled.[1]

2. Tom Wright, Lecturer in New Testament Studies at Oxford
University, in an essay *Jerusalem in the New Testament*, writing on
'all Israel will be saved' says:

Does this refer to a...large-scale...salvation of all Jews (or nearly all)? *No, it does not.* (Italics mine.)
Paul is clearly offering a deliberately polemical redefinition of Israel.[2]

Later in the essay he continues:

There is no justification, therefore, for taking Romans 11...as a prediction of a large scale, last minute salvation of Jews.[3]

3. James Dunn, Lightfoot Professor of Divinity at the University of Durham, in his Commentary on Romans, writing on 11:15 says:

the final act of salvation is also mediated through Israel...will only come through God's once again taking Israel to himself. The final act of all history rests upon the Jews.[4]

On 'all Israel will be saved' he writes:

The climax will be the fulfilment of his heart's prayer—Israel's salvation, Israel's restoration to full communion with its God. Israel would be saved by...abandoning their unbelief in Jesus as their Messiah in acceptance of the gospel.[5]

If readers want to know how such people, committed as they are to Scripture, come to such divergent views, they will need to dig more deeply into the above books than I can do here. Such problems can arise when letters such as Romans are approached with principles of prophecy and eschatology already determined, and the teaching of the letter has to fit in that framework.

This kind of thinking seems to be present in an earlier essay in 'Jerusalem Past and Present...' where Chris Wright knocks down a series of positions which none of us would wish to defend, in order to come to the conclusion:

In any case, nothing...requires or supports a national or territorial restoration of the Jews as being necessary in order to fulfil prophecy.[6]

In order to create a basis for an understanding of chapters 9–

11 we have to understand the framework of the opening chapters. We might summarise thus, following the outline given in the NIV Study Bible:

Chapter 2:28-29, which is often taken as a proof text that Christians are now the 'true Jews', is here seen in fact to be in a totally Jewish context. Paul is saying that the outward form of Judaism is not enough to make one righteous before God. Jews have to be inwardly righteous through spiritual renewal. The Hebrew root of 'Jew' means 'praise'. The end of verse 29 could be understood as 'Whose Judaism is not from men but from God'. (Arnold Fruchtenbaum)[8]. Christians (including Gentile Christians) are not part of the context of this section.

It is precisely because Paul takes this strong view of God's continuing faithfulness to his covenant with the Jewish People *as Jews* that chapters 9–11 were written. The apostle is, as it were, 'thinking aloud', working out his own bewilderment as he reconciles the knowledge that God has revealed to him the human reality of the state of his people which stared him in the face. If a so-called 'New Israel', comprising Jews and Gentiles who had turned to Christ, had come into being to replace national historical Israel, Paul might, through a sense of nostalgia and patriotism, have found this sad, but he would not have had to wrestle with the profound theological issues faced in chapters 9–11. Nor would he have come up with such radical solutions for the Jewish people as he does in this section.

If we are to understand the reasoning of Romans 9–11 correctly, we have first to realise that Paul is giving us a 'blow by blow account' of how he arrived at verses 2 and 25 of Chapter 11. The book of Acts and the New Testament letters are not, as we so often treat them, the authors' contribution to a long standing and ongoing debate about their meaning. We may, indeed we must life of God's people in every generation, but these documents were not written as contributions towards that debate. They were written as white hot revolutionary new truths from the heart of God by revelation of the Holy Spirit. We are not taking a 'mind-less fundamentalist' approach to them (whatever that might mean), but we need to recognise the nature of these documents and how and why they came into being if we are rightly to understand what they are saying. We shall not undertake a detailed study of this passage, but we will look at some of the difficult issues sometimes raised:

> It is not as though God's word had failed. For not all who are descended from Israel are Israel. Nor because they are his descendants are they all Abraham's children. On the contrary, 'It is through Isaac that your offspring will be reckoned.' In other words, it is not the natural children who are God's children, but it is the children of the promise who are regarded as Abraham's offspring (Rom 9:6-8).

As we have seen, these verses are sometimes expounded as meaning that physical, racial Jewishness was of no further relevance. It is sometimes said that these verses are the point at which Paul came, perhaps reluctantly, to that conclusion. Here again we have to look at the wider context.

Paul is wrestling with what he believes to be true about the Israel he sees before his eyes. Laying aside those thousands who had come to faith in Jerusalem and elsewhere, Paul sees his people in their corporate entity, especially the leadership body, as having rejected Jesus as their Messiah. He must also have had in his heart and mind those thriving Gentile churches he had founded throughout Asia Minor and Eastern Europe, though we must resist the temptation to idealise them.

Paul himself seems to be tempted towards a replacement theology solution, but as he argues with God it becomes clear that however great God's purposes are for a universal church incorporating Jew and Gentile as one people in Christ, this does not replace Israel as identifiable physical Israel. Israel is not just a 'stage on the way' to something greater in the purposes of God; a kind of chrysalis out of which the new, greater, spiritual Israel emerges.

However much Paul would have had to wrestle with his own feelings about this, if this was really the conclusion he had come to, then it seems inconceivable that he would have wrapped this truth up in such a way as we see in Romans 9–11. Paul was a man whose aim was always to present the truth plainly, without fear or favour, and if we take the great theme titles of Israel, Jew, Gentile, etc in their literal, physical, historical meanings, this in fact will give the simplest and most coherent explanation of this and other related passages in the Scriptures.

There is general agreement among scientists and mathematicians that there is an inherent simplicity in creation, and that the simplest hypothesis is most likely to be nearest the truth. In theology, the Queen of Sciences, the same holds true. This does not mean that there are not problems in interpreting these Scriptures, nor that we are not dealing with truths which ultimately are beyond the human mind fully to comprehend. We are dealing with a mystery, but in the language of the New Testament a 'mysterion' is not something that is incomprehensible; it is a truth that has just been revealed, a truth that could not have been arrived at by human reason! Paul uses the word 15 times, and each time the context is of clarity and explanation of revelation.

Sometimes the mystery has eschatological (end-times) significance.

> And he made known to us the mystery of his will according to his good pleasure, which he purposed in Christ, to be put into effect when the times will have reached their fulfilment—to bring all things in heaven and on earth together under one head, even Christ (Eph 1:9,10).

> Listen, I tell you a mystery: We will not all sleep, but we will all be changed (1 Cor 15:51).

Sometimes it has more immediate relevance.

> Pray also for me, that whenever I open my mouth, words may be given me so that I will fearlessly make known the mystery of the gospel (Eph 6:19).

As regards the mystery of Jew and Gentile, Israel and the

Church, there are both present and future applications. There is the present mystery of Gentiles coming to faith:

> The mystery that has been kept hidden for ages and generations, but is now disclosed to the saints. To them God has chosen to make known among the Gentiles the glorious riches of this mystery, which is Christ in you, the hope of glory (Col 1:26,27).

There is the present mystery of the Gentiles becoming heirs together with Israel. This is such a radical revelation that Paul has to use the word 'mysterion' 3 times in 4 verses, (Eph 3:3-6).

There is the mystery of Israel's hardening in part until the full number of Gentiles has come in, grafted as wild olive shoots into the natural olive tree of Israel (Rom 11:25), leading to the future mystery of the salvation of all Israel (11:26). If Paul were not speaking about natural, physical, historic Israel, then sections such as 11:28-31 would be just 'red herrings', totally redundant, meaningless complications in what he was saying.

If historic Israel had now served its purposes in the plan of God, whether faithfully or ignominiously it matters not, then Paul would have had absolutely no reason to make a major return to this theme in the conclusion of the practical application of his letter in Chapter 15:7-13

> Accept one another, then, just as Christ accepted you, in order to bring praise to God. For I tell you that Christ has become a servant of the Jews on behalf of God's truth, to confirm the promises made to the patriarchs so that the Gentiles may glorify God for his mercy, as it is written: 'Therefore I will praise you among the Gentiles; I will sing hymns to your name.' Again, it says, 'Rejoice, O Gentiles, with his people.' And again, 'Praise the Lord, all you Gentiles, and sing praises to him, all you peoples.' And again, Isaiah says, 'The Root of Jesse will spring up, one who will arise to rule over the nations; the Gentiles will hope in him.' May the God of hope fill you with all joy and peace as you trust in him, so that you may overflow with hope by the power of the Holy Spirit.

If it were God's plan to eradicate the Jew-Gentile distinctive within the body of Christ, then it would be very strange for Paul to be keeping it very much alive!

In the light of this, and what I have said about the earlier chapters of Romans, we can now go back to some of the other themes of Chapters 9–11 in order to throw light on them. Incontrovertibly Chapter 9 is a difficult chapter, but then it is dealing with one example of a major theme that, at every level, is beyond the mind of man to comprehend, namely the sovereignty of God and the freewill of man. This is a doctrine that Christians have agonised over, argued over, fallen out over, and attempted to hold in a creative tension, throughout Church history.

With this background it would seem that most commentators on Romans, having 'spiritualised' Chapters 2–4, now find it necessary to try to defend God against the charge of failure and unfairness by some kind of allegorical and spiritualised inter-pretation of this chapter also. They take 'Israel' to mean historic Israel, and 'Abraham's children' to mean his physical descen-dants, *in those parts where the text has failure in mind,* and to mean 'spiritual Israel' and Abraham's 'offspring according to faith', *where the chapter has righteousness in mind.*

God does not need this kind of defence. One is reminded of those chapter and section headings on old Victorian family and lectern bibles where, if Israel had done something bad, or some-thing strong had been prophesied against Israel, the heading was something like 'God's judgment is pronounced against the Jews', but if it was something good, then the heading would indicate 'The prophet speaketh of the glory of the Church that is to come'.

How should we interpret such passages as Romans 9:1-9?

I speak the truth in Christ–I am not lying, my conscience con-firms it in the Holy Spirit–I have great sorrow and unceasing anguish in my heart. For I could wish that I myself were cursed and cut off from Christ for the sake of my brothers, those of my own race, the people of Israel. Theirs is the adoption as sons; theirs the divine glory, the covenants, the receiving of the law, the temple worship and the promises. Theirs are the patriarchs, and from them is traced the human ancestry of Christ, who is God over all, forever praised! Amen. It is not as though God's word had failed. For not all who are descended from Israel are Israel. Nor because they are his descendants are they all Abraham's children. On the contrary, 'It is through Isaac that your offspring will be reckoned.' In other words, it is not the natural children who are

God's children, but it is the children of the promise who are regarded as Abraham's offspring. For this was how the promise was stated: 'At the appointed time I will return, and Sarah will have a son.'

First we need to recognise from the opening five verses, as we did in the analysis of Chapter 3, that the context is entirely Jewish, and as Paul's reasoning develops, however we may come to understand it, we need to interpret it in that context. From this we understand the following truths:

i) Not all of Abraham's offspring are children in the line of the covenant, because the covenant line is through Isaac and Jacob.

ii) Not all of Abraham's offspring are children in the line of the covenant, because they were not conceived by Abraham with covenant faith.

This puts Ishmael out on both counts, first because of the elective line that God chose, and secondly because of the manipulative action of Abraham and Sarah that led to his conception.

We need to interpret this passage in the clear and natural light of Genesis 21, to which it refers. Ishmael is called the 'natural' child, not because he was conceived by natural biological means (which of course he was), but because he was conceived as the result of a 'gruesome threesome' of scheming people trying to do God's work for him. On the other hand Isaac is called the child of promise, not because he was conceived by other than normal biological means (which of course he wasn't) but because his natural biological conception was, against all biological expectations, effected by the sovereign will and intervention of God.

The result to which Paul's reasoning is pointing is exactly the same as the one made in Chapter 2:28,29; true Jewishness, based, as it is, on physical descendency from Abraham, requires a reflection of Abraham's faithful response to God's covenant love. Romans 9:1-29 is entirely in a Jewish context. The question of where this leaves God's faithfulness to the Gentiles is not addressed until verse 30, which makes it abundantly clear that they also have found a righteousness which comes by faith; the same quality of faith that Abraham showed, but that must not be read into the previous historical section. That would be to confuse the way God has worked and is working. To allegorise the Old Testament at the expense of seeing it primarily as an historical record of God's dealing with a real people with whom he had made a covenant relationship, is tantamount to depersonalising this people.

We shall not look at Romans 9:10-26 in detail. Suffice it say that it deals, as previously indicated, with the tension of God's sovereignty and human freewill.

In conclusion we need to consider two further themes in Romans, namely priority and alleged favouritism.

In Chapter 1:16 Paul speaks of a priority of the Gospel for the Jewish people. The plain use of language here demands that we understand the two racial groups: there is no room here for any kind of 'spiritualising'. We have to ask 'Why the Jewish priority?' Is it, as is often alleged, favouritism of Jews by God. This charge is often made as a simple attempt at rejecting the whole thesis we have sought to establish in this chapter. Paul was already aware of this possibility: it is something that in all probability he had to face in his own time, and he answered the charge in Romans 2:7-11

> To those who by persistence in doing good seek glory, honour and immortality, he will give eternal life. But for those who are self-seeking and who reject the truth and follow evil, there will be wrath and anger. There will be trouble and distress for every human being who does evil: *first for the Jew*, then for the Gentile; but glory, honour and peace for everyone who does good: *first for the Jew*, then for the Gentile. *For God does not show favouritism.*

Not only is the gospel first for the Jew, but so is judgment. This is not favouritism; it is quite simply the inevitable demand and outworking of the Jewish people as still the covenant people of God. In the plan of God they are the people who will receive the salvation that comes through faith in the Jewish Messiah (Jesus), and they are the people who will bring the knowledge of salvation to the rest of the world. But in the mystery of the outworking of this plan, some words of Jesus came true here also, namely that 'the first shall be last, and the last first'. But ultimately God's plan cannot be thwarted, and the Jews also shall find salvation.

As far as the gospel is concerned, they are enemies on your account; but as far as election is concerned, they are loved on account of the patriarchs, for God's gifts and his call are irrevocable. Just as you who were at one time disobedient to God have now received mercy as a result of their disobedience, so they too have now become disobedient in order that they too may now receive mercy as a result of God's mercy to you. For God has bound all men over to disobedience so that he may have mercy on them all. Oh, the depth of the riches of the wisdom and knowledge of God! How unsearchable his judgments, and his paths beyond tracing out! 'Who has known the mind of the Lord? Or who has been his counsellor?' 'Who has ever given to God, that God should repay him?' For from him and through him and to him are all things. To him be the glory forever! Amen (Rom 11:28-36).

The need for salvation is equal and identical for Jew and for Gentile. We are all 'bound over to disobedience.' The way of salvation is identical for Jew and for Gentile, 'The power of the gospel' (1:16). The fruit of salvation is identical for Jew and for Gentile, in that both are justified through faith, both are no longer under condemnation, both have peace with God, both are heirs of eternal life. In this sense Galatians 3:28 comes true:

There is neither Jew nor Greek, slave nor free, male nor female, for you are all one in Christ Jesus.

But that unity in Christ does not mean *uniformity*. The unity of God is the corporate 'three in one'. The mystery of humankind made in the image of God is Genesis 1:27.

So God created man in his own image, in the image of God he created him; male and female he created them.

The mystery is unity in diversity; complementariness in unity. 'Neither male nor female', when they plainly do exist, is a paradox that we are learning to live with in creative tension in the Church today. We need to learn the same creative tension with Jew and Gentile.

It is a tragedy that the human spirit of competitiveness seems constantly to dog Jewish-Christian relationships. From a human point of view the reasons are understandable. Jews feel that

Christians claim to have superseded them in the purposes of God. Christians feel that the Jews claim to priority leads to a spirit of elitism. Messianic Jews often feel in the middle and accused by both sides! These things may be understandable, but they are inexcusable among the children of God. As Paul comes to the end of Chapter 11, it almost seems that he is anticipating the danger signals as he ends on a great paean of praise–'Oh, the depths of the wisdom of God...'

What is the basis of that praise? That we all stand equal before God. What is the basis of our equality? Not, as many humanists wish to affirm today, our common human dignity, but, as Paul expresses it, our common disobedience. And the end product? That God might have mercy upon us all.

CHAPTER 9

I Knew it was Jesus.
Stuart and Lori

I HAD THE PLEASURE OF visiting Stuart and Lori, and their lovely family, one evening, so that they could share their story with me. Their four children took their big black collie for a walk, so that we could drink coffee and chat.

Lori: I grew up in a very middle-class Jewish family in Chicago in the USA, where we had a lovely house in a very Jewish neighbourhood. Though we belonged to a Reformed Synagogue, my parents weren't particularly religious, attending only for some of the Festivals. Also I went to Jewish Sunday School and was very keen to learn the history of my people.

Stuart: I was brought up in St John's Wood, London, a very Jewish community. My grandparents and my great-aunts also lived there. They went to the West London Orthodox Synagogue and my parents fitted in with them. We moved out to Stanmore when I was about eleven years old, and started going to a Reformed Synagogue. It was a good family and home background, Jewish, without being particularly spiritual. We took for granted that there was a God but we didn't actually talk about it. I became Bar Mitzvah at Edgware Reformed Synagogue and at that time was really quite keen. I went to boarding school in Seaford, Sussex from about 7, and later on to Brighton College, where my closest friends were Jewish, but I didn't mix with many other Jewish people in Stanmore or in London. We used to go to *shul* fairly regularly as a family which I enjoyed less as I grew older because I was beginning to search and to find it unsatisfying.

Lori: When I was about thirteen or fourteen, my parents divorced. I actually had an awareness of God and I used to pray to him, but somehow he was very distant. I went into the Synagogue on my own once, and sat in the main hall: I was very aware of God's holiness. But somehow after that I went through a typical teenage rebellion. My parents accepted it; they weren't really that religious themselves.

Stuart: My parents also split up in the late sixties. At that time it was more the exception than now, and I was absolutely shattered. I was sixteen and had no idea that it was coming. I was having problems at school, a growing unhappiness: I just wanted freedom from school and restrictions. By the time I left school, I had already determined the course of action that I was going to take. I had become quite good at art (my mother was an artist) and my aim in life was to become a hippy. I left school halfway through my A levels course, went to art college in Harrow, and from there to St Martin's Art College in London. By then I was on a downhill spiral. I got involved with all the wrong people, drugs, and all that went with it.

Incidentally, the first Christian I ever met was at art college; he showed me a Francis Schaeffer book, but I couldn't make head or tail of it! I can still remember what the cover looked like. I was beginning to feel that being a Jew was somehow irrelevant, and I was quite happy to leave it all behind because I found it difficult and very constricting. My one thought was freedom.

Lori: The late sixties, early seventies was a time when a lot of young people were searching. A lot of my friends were searching for something. That was the hippy time and a lot of the hippies were talking about peace, love, joy, kindness etc. It was a new way of living, as against the old way of the Establishment. Although I had lots of friends around me, there was still something inside me that felt very alone and empty. Some of my friends and also my brother got involved in drugs. I tried them but I had a bad experience once, and decided to have nothing more to do with them.

I knew there must be something more to life than just getting married, having children and going to work. I searched, but I didn't know for what. When I finished high school I went on to college at Santa Cruz, just south of San Francisco. I tried transcendental meditation, then Buddhism, and I read up books on different philosophies, eastern religions and the occult.

My major subject at college was English and I was also very

interested in studying the American Indians, and got into quite a lot of their religious ideas, very New Age, Mother Earth and the Great Spirit. One of our teachers challenged us to ask this Great Spirit for a vision like the Indians used to do, so I went away and prayed on a hill, Red Indian style, and the amazing thing was that I saw in a vision, an outline of a shining man in the distance. I don't know how or why, but I knew it was Jesus. I knew from the vision that he was coming back to the world for sinners. I didn't really know much of the Bible. I hadn't heard a lot about Jesus, and what I knew about him was from films.

Stuart: I was more interested in philosophy, poetry and art. I got more and more heavily involved in the drug scene, but then, through a whole series of experiences I became very disenchanted. I look back with a great deal of regret, shame, and repentance over the things I was involved in. I was in darkness, often really miserable and depressed. Whenever I could, I used to travel in England and abroad, and from time to time I would slip into a church because something seemed to draw me there, and I would just cry.

Eventually I went to Exeter University where I studied English and Art. I drifted in and out of everything I did, and didn't complete that course either. I was aware that there was a spiritual sense to the universe; there had to be something other than what I was involved in.

I had totally written off Judaism at this stage. I started getting interested in Eastern religions, which is a natural extension of a rejection of Christianity or Judaism and being involved in the drug world. I became quite involved in Hinduism, had a guru, a chap who was involved with the United Nations Organisation. I used to go round in white; everything had to be white. I nearly joined Hari Krishna. I found a natural affinity with Hinduism, because it seemed to be a path of holiness, and it seemed like some sort of answer. But this guru wasn't what I thought he would be. He gave us a test. He said, 'I want you to look into your heart to see who is really most important there.' He was expecting us all to say that he was, as we were all his closest disciples, and most of the other guys said that he was; he was the guru. However, when I looked into my heart, there was one name that was there more strongly than any other; the name of Jesus.

I had met people who had witnessed to me; I had said I was an atheist. Even though I argued aggressively with them, I can see now just how effective their witness was. One night a German student gave me a lift in his Volkswagen, and spent the whole time telling me about Jesus—I was not impressed!

Throughout that time, as a Jew who was very far away from my roots and far away from anything rabbinical at all, the person of Jesus was an attractive enigma. I knew he was a Jew, an outsider, and somehow a holy man. There was something of a mystery about him.

When I was studying art, we went to the Victoria and Albert museum and I happened to sit down underneath a beautiful mediaeval half life size statue of Jesus. After I had been there for about two hours, I suddenly became aware of this statue and of a sense of power there, even though it was only a statue. I just had to keep looking at it. I knew enough of the story, which I had probably learnt at school because we had to sit through Scripture classes, and I reached my hand up to the wounded side and remembered Thomas: it was a strange experience.

Lori: After I had the vision of Jesus, although I sort of believed in him, I didn't really understand what I was supposed to do about it. I met a young man at college who was a Christian, and he told me about Jesus. I told him that I was Jewish, meaning that Jesus is for Gentiles but not for Jews. He said to me that for a Jewish person to believe in Jesus was a double blessing, and although I didn't understand what he meant, somehow that phrase stayed with me. He also told me that all the early disciples were Jews. I never knew that, in fact I knew very little about Jesus, and a lot of what I had heard was untrue. In any case I didn't like the popular image of Christians very much.

In my second year at college I was asked by my best friend if I would like to go on a holiday to Europe, to England, which is an American dream, and the two of us came for the summer.

In England I met Stuart, who at that time was a friend of the people with whom we stayed. It was during this time that I picked up the Bible and started reading it. There was something about the Psalms that comforted my heart.

Within a couple of months Stuart had asked me to marry him. We got engaged and wondered where we would go to get married. Stuart's mother suggested the Synagogue that she knew. It was a fairly new Reformed Synagogue which didn't have its own premises, so the congregation met in a church. One day Stuart picked up a couple of books at the back, one of which was a Good News for Modern Man, a Bible in modern English, and he brought it home.

I started to read it and couldn't put it down. It was like food for my hungry soul. When I read about Jesus, I was just amazed at the fact that his life took place in Israel and that he lived among Jews, and was called Rabbi. His teaching was unlike any other sort of teaching I had ever come across. I was totally fascinated by him; what a wonderful person he was.

When I started to read the Letter to the Romans, especially chapters 9 to 11, I suddenly realised that Jesus was the Jewish Messiah. It all made sense to me that he came to our people and they rejected him; that the Gentiles would then embrace him as their Lord and Saviour, but that later on the Jews would believe in him again. It was as if the central piece of a jigsaw puzzle that had been missing was suddenly put into place, and I just knew that he was the Messiah.

One day I went into my room to pray to God as my Father about a small problem and as I was in my room praying I just felt the presence of Jesus there. It was like when you tune a radio and suddenly Radio 4 comes over loud and clear. Suddenly Jesus was there. I didn't see him, but I just knew he was there. I said 'I'm home, I've found you, I don't have to look any more'. I knew that I wasn't alone any more, that Jesus knew all about me, what was inside me, what I thought, and what I felt, and a tremendous comfort and peace flooded me.

I think that was the time that I was born again, because from that moment on I sought out other Christians. Stuart was also becoming a believer about the same time, but I really thought that we were the only two crazy Jews who believed that Jesus was the Messiah!

Stuart: When I met Lori, I was still painting. I had left the drug scene not long before, but I was very disillusioned with eastern religions, and was really at the end of myself.

After we met I wanted to find my roots and became interested in Judaism again. I was beginning to feel a need to belong and that was why we decided to get married in the Reformed Synagogue. At the same time we were seeing something in the New Testament that was totally new and different, and we weren't quite sure where it was leading us. I had absolutely no desire to become a Christian because I felt it was a narrow blinkered existence, though I felt that I might believe in this person Jesus.

When we visited Lori's family in America her mother said, as a very typical open-minded Californian Jewish mother, 'Why don't you visit "Jews for Jesus"?' We hadn't the faintest idea what 'Jews for Jesus' was, but we went. I was really attracted to them as people, but put off by what I thought was a very narrow-minded way of life. I was very confused.

When we came back to England I found for the first time in years I couldn't do the art which had been my prop; the one thing which had given me some kind of sanity. I spent two weeks trying to do a drawing and couldn't. I felt as if I was being confronted by a wall that was spreading around me and not letting me through. At the end of about two weeks I realised that the wall I was facing was somehow the Lord. I new what I had to do; I had to give up my art, the one thing that had really been a crutch to me.

I had amassed quite a volume of work by then. I made a decision to follow Jesus as my Lord and Saviour. I went out and burned all my art work and completely cut myself off from it. I thought I would never take it up again. But I had found the Lord.

It was a very shaky beginning and for the next two years was quite a battle coming to an understanding of this totally new life. I had thought that in my search I had found freedom, but soon realised that I was more and more in chains. Everything I thought that I was, I found I wasn't; somehow I had amassed all the wrong values. I had worked hard at being a rebel for so many years, and had suffered for my rebellion.

God really made us whole and radically changed us in the first year or two that we became believers. As soon as we became believers we had an immediate love for the Jewish People. I had never had that before. In my wildest dreams I had never thought that I would be a lover of Israel and the Jewish People. I had felt for years a total antipathy for Jews and wanted to be as far away as I could from the Jewish community. But now we had an immediate burden for our own people, that they would come to know the Lord and Messiah.

Lori: When I found the Lord I experienced real happiness and joy for the first time in my life, whereas before I was often quite lonely and thought that nobody could understand me completely. Now I felt that Jesus really understood everything about me and I could share everything with him, That was a tremendous comfort to me and life started to take on a whole new meaning. I also came to understand my need for repentance over the wrong things I had done and going my own way.

As we read the Bible more, and started to go to church, we began to understand more about what it was to be a follower of Jesus. We also met other Jewish Christians and began to seek them out and have Bible studies with them, which was very helpful to us. For the first time in my life I started to understand not only what it means to be a Christian, but also what it means to be a Jew. Now I was very thankful that God had made me Jewish and that he had a purpose for my life, and I knew that the history of the Jewish people was planned by God.

CHAPTER 10

We Who are Jews by Birth.
Paul's Letter to the Galatians

P AUL'S LETTER TO THE Church in Galatia is frequently
used to show that any holding on to Jewish practices by
Christians of Jewish origin is a holding on to the bondage
of legalism, and therefore a challenge to the doctrine of 'grace and
faith'. This was a view held by a number of the Early Church
Fathers. It was certainly a view clearly held by Martin Luther
and is still not uncommon in the church today. How valid is this?

In order to interpret a book of the Bible correctly, we need to
ask first 'What kind of book is this? Who wrote it? When was it
written? Where was it written? Why was it written?'

This is important, and probably its importance is not greater
in any document than this letter to the Galatians. This kind of
questioning in no way detracts from the fundamental evangelical
doctrine of the inspiration of Scripture, rather it enhances it. We
believe that God used people, circumstances and situations in
order to reveal his word. What we are doing when we ask these
kind of questions does not relate to the doctrine of inspiration so
much as to our methods of interpretation. I do not intend to play
down the importance of systematic theology when I say that the
biblical records are not systematic theology. In fact systematic
theology, as we know it, is a Greek rather than a Jewish discipline, and in the Bible we are dealing with the writings of predominantly Jewish authors. This is not to say that systematic
theology is not of great importance, but we need to recognise that
there are questions to be asked and answered, and problems to be
resolved before we can turn biblical writings into systematic
theology. If we don't do this effectively, we shall find ourselves
giving way to the frequently levelled, but false idea, that Scrip-

ture contradicts itself; or we shall come to false deductions and wrong applications of Scripture to situations we are facing.

CIRCUMCISION

Let us look at the subject of circumcision as an example, from a variety of Paul's writings.

> Circumcision is nothing and uncircumcision is nothing. Keeping God's commands is what counts (1 Cor 7:19).

> For in Christ Jesus neither circumcision nor uncircumcision has any value. The only thing that counts is faith expressing itself through love (Gal 5:6).

> Brothers, if I am still preaching circumcision, why am I still being persecuted? In that case the offence of the cross has been abolished (Gal 5:11).

> ...though I myself have reasons for such confidence. If anyone else thinks he has reasons to put confidence in the flesh, I have more: circumcised on the eighth day, of the people of Israel, of the tribe of Benjamin, a Hebrew of Hebrews; in regard to the law, a Pharisee; as for zeal, persecuting the church; as for legalistic righteousness, faultless. But whatever was to my profit I now consider loss for the sake of Christ. What is more, I consider everything a loss compared to the surpassing greatness of knowing Christ Jesus my Lord, for whose sake I have lost all things. I consider them rubbish, that I may gain Christ (Phil 3:4-8).

> There is neither Jew nor Greek, slave nor free, male nor female, for you are all one in Christ Jesus (Gal 3:28).

> Was a man already circumcised when he was called? He should not become uncircumcised. Was a man uncircumcised when he was called? He should not be circumcised (1 Cor 7:18).

Yet Paul had Timothy circumcised, as we saw in chapter 6, and he could write:

> What advantage, then, is there in being a Jew, or what value is there in circumcision? Much in every way! First of all, they have been entrusted with the very words of God (Rom 3:1,2).

It is clear from the last example that Paul was not against

circumcision, only its abuse. He was not against a Jew who came to faith in Jesus continuing to identify and practise as a Jew: indeed to the end of his recorded ministry he maintained that claim for himself.

> Then Paul made his defence: 'I have done nothing wrong against the law of the Jews or against the temple or against Caesar.' (Acts 25:8).

The corrective for wrong use is not disuse but right use. We have to understand that circumcision is the sign and seal of two covenants in the Hebrew Scriptures. The first is the Abrahamic covenant where circumcision is given as a sign of God's everlasting covenant with the physical lineage of Abraham, Isaac and Jacob, the Jewish people. As Paul emphasises

> The law, introduced 430 years later, does not set aside the covenant previously established by God and thus do away with the promise (Gal 3:17).

This is the significance of Timothy's circumcision, and it is the basis for the validity of the practice of circumcision, as an option, not a mandate, amongst Messianic Jews today.

The second covenant sealed by the sign of circumcision is the Mosaic Covenant in which the Jewish people were given the Torah on Mount Sinai. As we have noted elsewhere, Torah observance was never intended to be a 'works-righteousness' covenant, but, beginning with the Babylonian captivity, and going into other situations where Jewish communities were established far from Jerusalem, and therefore far from the Temple sacrifices, the temptation was to make Torah observance a substitute for sacrificial atonement.

It is in this context that the Judaizers were seeking to bring Gentile Christians under the bondage of the law, that is, bringing people who had been justified by God's grace, received through faith in Jesus' atoning sacrifice, into the bondage of a system of works righteousness which had never been intended for them.

THE REASON FOR WRITING

Why was the letter to the Galatians written? There is an immediate link in situation and subject matter with Acts 15 and the problems which the Council of Jerusalem was called to address.

> ...False brothers had infiltrated our ranks to spy on the freedom we have in Christ Jesus... (Gal 2:4).

Compare this with

> Some men came down from Judea to Antioch and were teaching the brothers 'Unless you are circumcised, according to the custom taught by Moses, you cannot be saved' (Acts 15:1).

> I would like to learn just one thing from you: Did you receive the Spirit by observing the law, or by believing what you heard? (Gal 3:2).

Compare this with

> He made no distinction between us and them, for he purified their hearts by faith (Acts 15:9).

This letter was written because of the false teaching of the Judaizers: the attempt to turn Gentiles into Jews in order to receive them as Christians. It is in this context that the letter was written, and must be understood. If we feel that this is not a relevant topic for today, we must use our imaginations, engage in a little 'lateral thinking' which is in fact a very Jewish thing to do, and at least two parallel issues come to mind.

The first, and for our purposes, most important issue, is the pressure now put on the predominantly Gentile church to pressurise Jews into becoming Gentiles, or at least give up an identifiably Jewish lifestyle, in order to become followers of (a very Jewish) Jesus. I have been quite severely taken to task by respected Church leaders when I have let it be known that our congregation meets on the Sabbath (Saturday).

The other point is the degree of petty legalism that often creeps into church practice and lifestyle, which we Jews often find more oppressive in the church we are invited to join than in the synagogue we are urged to leave! This is not now as great as it used to be. I well remember the taboo on alcohol and dancing, which was presented as though it were a biblical prohibition. Obviously the views of abstainers need to be respected, and there needs to be wisdom, moderation, and tolerance, but these are sometimes as lacking in the church as in the synagogue.

ABRAHAM'S OFFSPRING

So often the teaching of this letter is related to the question of whether Christians (of whatever origin, Gentile or Jew) are the true children of Abraham, rather than the Jewish People by race. If Paul had been dealing with *that* question he would have written very differently. We must beware using those Scriptures which answer a particular issue being addressed by the writer, to answer different questions which may be urgently at the forefront of our minds. We will find our answers by digging deeply, by looking at contexts, by comparing Scripture with Scripture, but short cuts will, as they so often have, lead us into error. So, with Paul, let us 'consider Abraham'.

> Consider Abraham: 'He believed God, and it was credited to him as righteousness.' Understand, then, that those who believe are children of Abraham. The Scripture foresaw that God would justify the Gentiles by faith, and announced the gospel in advance to Abraham: 'All nations will be blessed through you.' So those who have faith are blessed along with Abraham, the man of faith.... He redeemed us in order that the blessing given to Abraham might come to the Gentiles through Christ Jesus, so that by faith we might receive the promise of the Spirit (Gal 3:6-9,14).

Gentiles who come to faith in Jesus, become 'children of Abraham'; that is not in doubt. But we still have to ask 'in what way and how?' 'Child of' or 'son of' can mean either the biological offspring of someone, or 'bearing the likeness of or reflecting the qualities of', in the way Judas is called literally 'the son of perdition' in John 17:12 (KJV). It is clear that Paul is not suggesting that Gentile believers become children of Abraham in a biological sense, but in the sense of sharing the same faith and spiritual character. How this happens is not answered in this letter, it was not relevant to the occasion. But we do find the answer in Romans 11, 'by being grafted into the Jewish olive tree'.

In Galatians Paul is writing to Gentile Christians who are under pressure to take on submission to the Jewish law in order to gain salvation. *The standing of Jewish believers in Jesus is not relevant to this letter, and nothing written here can be directly applied to their context.*

> Mark my words! I, Paul, tell you that if you let yourselves be circumcised, Christ will be of no value to you at all. Again I declare to every man who lets himself be circumcised that he is obligated to obey the whole law (Gal 5:2,3).

How do we square this strong statement with Paul's having Timothy circumcised and then with 1 Corinthians 7:18?

> Was a man already circumcised when he was called? He should not become uncircumcised. Was a man uncircumcised when he was called? He should not be circumcised.

And then with Romans 2:25

> Circumcision has value if you observe the law, but if you break the law, you have become as though you had not been circumcised.

This is the only way that we can bring harmony and consistency into the breadth of the biblical teaching, especially as we see it in Paul's life and teaching, whilst at the same time keeping a consistency of interpretation of the words 'Jew', 'Israel' etc. and not subjectively interpreting them as sometimes meaning 'the physical race', and sometimes 'the Church', because we have already approached the passages with our own false preconceptions.

THE COVENANT WITH ABRAHAM

We now approach the admittedly difficult passage of Galatians 4:21-31.

> Tell me, you who want to be under the law, are you not aware of what the law says? For it is written that Abraham had two sons,

one by the slave woman and the other by the free woman. His son by the slave woman was born in the ordinary way; but his son by the free woman was born as the result of a promise. These things may be taken figuratively, for the women represent two covenants. One covenant is from Mount Sinai and bears children who are to be slaves: This is Hagar. Now Hagar stands for Mount Sinai in Arabia and corresponds to the present city of Jerusalem, because she is in slavery with her children. But the Jerusalem that is above is free, and she is our mother. For it is written: 'Be glad, O barren woman, who bears no children; break forth and cry aloud, you who have no labour pains; because more are the children of the desolate woman than of her who has a husband.' Now you, brothers, like Isaac, are children of promise. At that time the son born in the ordinary way persecuted the son born by the power of the Spirit. It is the same now. But what does the Scripture say? 'Get rid of the slave woman and her son, for the slave woman's son will never share in the inheritance with the free woman's son.' Therefore, brothers, we are not children of the slave woman, but of the free woman.

This passage is frequently interpreted to mean that the Church is the true inheritor of the Covenant made with Abraham, Isaac and Jacob, ie it is the 'New Israel', while the Jews, who are in fact the true descendants, are said to be the spiritual descendants of Hagar. Not only is this a wrong interpretation, it is a seriously wrong interpretation, and lies at the root of so much Christian antisemitism, both among the Early Church Fathers, and in Martin Luther's Reformation teaching, which has infected much Protestant teaching since.

Paul says he is 'writing figuratively', so it is valid, in fact it is important that we understand him in this way. In Jewish terminology, as David Stern translates it in his 'Jewish New Testament' Paul is making a Midrash.[1] God's covenant through the son of the free woman (Isaac-Sarah) was with a view to bringing the promise of freedom into the world. God's covenant with Moses was with a view to bringing bondage and the knowledge of sin into the world. Figuratively this is the result of Abraham's 'affair' with Hagar.

Paul is saying in this Midrash that the way of freedom is the way of Abraham with Sarah, that is faith in the promises of God, while the way of Abraham with Hagar is the way of bondage. The

Torah was given to bring knowledge of sin, and by so doing to bring those who were under conviction of sin through the law to an experience of salvation through faith in the Messiah. But the Messiah also is Jewish, the Church which he created by the outpouring of the Holy Spirit was totally in a Jewish context for perhaps the first ten years of its existence. Gentile believers were included by expansion, not by replacement.

All this, for Jew and Gentile alike, has been an act of God's grace from beginning to end. Gentiles must not be squeezed into a Jewish mould, but neither do Jewish believers have to have their Jewishness erased. God's purpose is that in his time Israel will be saved.

Until that time comes it is important that there exists a remnant of Israel which believes in the Messiah who will bring this about. It is therefore also important that all Christians understand the nature and purpose of the Messianic Jewish position, and that we receive not only understanding but active and enthusiastic support.

CHAPTER 11

Through His own Jewish Eyes.
Martin Goldsmith

ONE FINE SPRING AFTERNOON I chatted with Martin in his home near All Nations Christian College in Hertfordshire. The sitting room was well decorated, not only with artifacts reflecting his worldwide travel and ministry, but also of his illustrious Jewish family pedigree. As we chatted, I became aware that I was in the presence of a man in the line of Solomon Goldschmidt, his great grandfather, whose small but powerful portrait hung above my head. As he shared his varied and adventurous life story I realised that here was a man who had struggled deeply for identity.

Martin's family was related by marriage to the merchant banking families of the Warburgs and the Rothschilds, Lord Samuel and the other Samuels. His grandparents came over from Germany and founded the metal exchange in London; there is a little plaque on the chair at the head of the boardroom table. Brandeis Goldschmidt was the family firm – Goldschmidt was his father, Brandeis was his cousin. The firm was eventually taken over by Mercury Securities, and now by the Warburgs, and so, in a sense, the firm has 'come home' again.

Religiously, Martin's father, as also his paternal uncles and aunts, were baptised as infants because his grandparents felt in coming to England they wanted their children to be really English. They weren't religious themselves, but felt to be really English included baptism and Church of England membership. His mother's parents were not religious but she was also baptised aged about seventeen in order to be English, so on both sides there was a strong sense of need for assimilation. Martin spoke of this traditional assimilation with a sense of understanding of the immense pressures behind it, though he does not see it as bring-

ing with it an entry into real Christian faith or a lessening of his
own Jewish identity..

In spite of their deeply worked-at assimilation, the family still
felt insecure, and moved to Bermuda for the duration of the war,
to escape Hitler, should he ever reach these shores. Martin was
about ten years old when the family returned to England. All
their furniture came out of storage but the one and only thing that
seemed to belong to him personally was a Bible which had been
given to him at his baptism. He began to read it and discovered
how amazingly Jewish it was. At the time he was at boarding
school near Manchester, and every evening they had a period of
supervised reading. While most of the boys were reading such
classics as Biggles, he read his Bible–not because he was religious
or pious, but out of sheer interest in the story it told. He read it
from cover to cover and was so fascinated that he went back to
the beginning again and kept doing this every year until he was
about twenty. The Bible was very much part of his life, but in an
historical and literary way, rather than a religious one.

There were other influences which made Martin aware of his
Jewishness. When he came back from Bermuda he met a distant
cousin who had come out of Germany, and had been in one of the
camps and had clearly suffered a great deal.

At the age of thirteen Martin went to Charterhouse and had
quite a bad time in his first two years through bullying which had
some antisemitic overtones. One time he was reading the Bible as
usual, and a thought came to him that the hero, God, seemed
right through the book to do amazing miracles to deliver his
people and save them from trouble. He prayed that God would
give him 24 hours in which nobody would say or do anything to
him, ie no bullying or teasing. And God, amazingly, took him
absolutely literally. No boy or teacher said or did anything to him
for 24 hours; no one said a word to him or asked him a question,
let alone bullied him. He even played football in the afternoon
and no one asked him to pass the ball.

At the end of 24 hours, amazed by what had happened, he
went to the Chapel. No one else was around. He stood at the top
of the steps leading down into the body of the Chapel, and in a
loud voice gave his life to God. God had proved himself and he
would follow him. From then on he set out to be 'religious'; he

went to Chapel regularly and got confirmed, but this was not the great success he hoped it would be, because it was done very much in his own strength rather than in the power of God. As Martin put it, 'I still hadn't appreciated the doctrine of justification by grace and the significance of the cross of Jesus.'

Two years service in the Royal Navy as a Russian interpreter interrupted Martin's academic career, though not God's continuing preparation for the life's ministry he was to fulfil. Though he joined the United Naval Christian Fellowship, his Christian life was lived very much with one foot still in the world.

After naval service Martin went to Oxford. On one occasion a student from the Christian Union invited him for a drink. Expecting, from his naval experience, something stronger, he was surprised to be offered Horlicks! The only person in the world he knew who drank Horlicks was a rather old great aunt of his. The meeting developed into a disastrous time of non-communication, and the student duly reported back to the CU that 'Goldsmith was hopeless'. Another student picked up the expression, and said, 'With God nobody is hopeless'. This student, Colin Jee, now an Anglican minister, got hold of him, and in his very unorthodox, direct manner of evangelism, won Martin. He shared with Martin that it wasn't what he did for God that counted, but what God had done for him in Christ.

Martin also came into contact with the Russian Orthodox Church, because of his Russian studies, and was very impressed by some of the Russian Orthodox monks who came to speak to them—people who had been alone with God for 20 or 30 years, who really knew God and themselves. This gave a spiritual depth to them, though doctrinally and biblically they might not have been altogether convincing. The combination of all these influences was very powerful and radically changed his life.

At the end of his first year at Oxford Martin felt God calling him into mission service overseas, so he went to what was then Clifton Theological College, now part of Trinity College, Bristol. At Clifton there came the feeling that Christianity was like a beautifully made jacket bought 'off the peg'; the material and cut were excellent, but it didn't quite fit on his shoulders. At the time he always felt that it was his shoulders that were wrong, but later he came to realise that maybe it was the coat that didn't fit him.

The coat was very Gentile and somehow didn't fit him culturally. Clifton gave him a superb foundation for his faith upon which he could build in later years, but he began to realise that the biblical and theological teaching he was receiving was very Gentile, mono-cultural and British.

It was at this point in our conversation that I began to realise a common strand running through many of the stories recorded in this book. England had provided a safe haven for the family. The witness of vibrant Christians had brought a living faith in Jesus. But there resulted an identity confusion which was reflected in the stories of others who had contributed, and I was eagerly looking forward to hearing how this was resolved. Many aspects of the problem were common to our experiences, but God's way of resolving them seemed to be unique to each one of us. We needed to pool our stories, not only with each other, but also within the wider body of the church, in order to see what God was doing with his people.

The Wycliffe Language Course was the next stage in Martin's preparation for service with the Overseas Missionary Fellowship. Here he met Elizabeth and, in his words 'began to pursue her'. Both went to Singapore in April 1960 and worked among Muslims. Martin found this very interesting from his Jewish perspective, because he found Islamic and Jewish culture to be so close. He found he had a natural affinity to Islam and to Muslims, and it was very easy to relate to them and to understand Islam.

There followed a mind blowing variety of ministries which included pioneer Muslim work in Singapore and South Thailand; a massive church growth situation in Indonesia within the Reformed Church, and then pastoring of a Chinese church in Malaysia. This latter was especially illuminating, because the overseas (non-China) Chinese were somewhat similar to Jews in that they shared the same insecurities and fear of oppression, the same desire to get on in the world and gain security in life. They developed the same family networks as Jews have in mutual responsibilities, duties and rights within the extended family. So Martin has always felt very much at home with the Chinese.

When he was in Indonesia, the churches he worked with had already been independent of missionary influence for some years. He found, almost for the first time in his life, a Christianity that fitted him like a good-fitting jacket on his shoulders, felt 'at home' as seldom before. Later, as he reflected on it, he realised that it was an Asian form of Christianity that was actually closer to Jewish ways than traditional Western approaches. He began to realise some of the Jewishness of his Christian faith and to see Scripture through his own Jewish eyes rather than through traditional Gentile eyes. This opened Scripture up in a new way for him and made the whole of the understanding and interpretation of the Scriptures come alive in a new way.

This somewhat surprising twist in events, not just that God should bring a Jew to faith and then lead him to share that faith with Muslims, but that this experience of Asian Christianity and culture should actually become the instrument by which Martin could begin to resolve the tension between his Jewish 'being' and his faith in Jesus, led me to meditate further on the ways of the Almighty. I realised how urgently we need to ask deep questions about the way the Church has not only 'westernised' a middle eastern faith (which to some extent may be acceptable for western Christians), but is then exporting the westernised article as though it were the original product.

As we talked further about this, Martin shared examples of his understanding of the New Testament as relating a 'Hebrew background Gospel' to a culturally and philosophically mixed world of Jew and Gentile. There is the need to address such questions as: 'How are we to understand the God of Israel as also the God of all the earth? How is the Jewish Messiah also the Christ of the Gentiles? How do the Gentiles fit into the Jewish root of the tree?'

Martin emphasised the importance of such points as 'Seeing the church with its foundation in the 'kahal' (the community and congregation) of Israel', which is hardly seen or addressed by Gentile writers.

In terms of spirituality there are a whole variety of things; the amazing ways that Jews have of being able to be almost frivolously humorous when being very serious, or being awfully serious when actually being humorous; being able to slip in worship from a good laugh and a vivacious dance into a really solemn Hebrew dirge and back again, without being irreverent. All this is part of Jewish culture, as is also communication that is much more direct, up-front and outrageous in many ways. He finds it sad that there has still never been a Jew asked to expound the Scriptures in any international Christian congress in this century, whether ecumenical, Roman Catholic or evangelical.

But is a 'westernised' Christianity all right for western peoples? How can a 'Jewish' Christianity (which is where Christianity began) be translated for another culture? Since in the Bible God reveals himself as the only God, and Jesus as the only Saviour of all people, this cultural translation must not only be possible, it is important and urgent. But how can this be done?

Martin finds that much of the Western approach to theology is totally un-Jewish in its way of thinking. The Gentile approach is linear and ontological. 'Take John 1 as an example,' he told me. 'Gentiles are very interested in who Jesus was; was he God, was he man, was he both etc. Jews however would be much more interested in what he did, that he was the creating word. I sympathise with the liberationist, though non-Jew, José Miranda, who translates John 1:1 as "In the beginning was communication, and communication was with God, and communication was actually God". What God does is what counts, and that is Jewish.'

With regard to Messianic Judaism, Martin's views have changed. 'If I had been asked 10 years ago I would have been quite opposed to forming homogeneous units or Jewish churches. Now I feel that because there is such a strong emphasis on 'you cannot be a Jew and a Christian', it is very important for Jewish identity to have churches which are Jewish in personnel and character. They demonstrate the reality of the fact that just as you can be English and Christian, so you can also be Jewish and Christian; and you don't lose your Christianity or Christian-ness, nor do you lose your Jewishness, any more than you lose your Englishness or Christian-ness in being an English Christian.'

Although Martin doesn't at the moment belong to a Messianic group, he thoroughly supports the principle of it, and feels it is an important testimony in our country and in the world. Whereas he was brought up in a very Gentile context and therefore fitted into the church reasonably easily, he empathises with his sisters and brothers who come from much more strongly Jewish contexts than he does, and who actually find the church very difficult to fit into.

When asked about 'Jews for Jesus', Martin told me that he is very pleased that they have come to England, and in fact is a member of the Board of 'Jews for Jesus'. He continued:

'They are going to be very important in Britain; they have a form of witness that is authentically Jewish. Most Christian witness is Gentile in character and never really scratches below the surface of Jews. I am very interested to see the church's reaction to 'Jews for Jesus', and the Jewish community's reaction. I would expect the latter to be over the top and virulent.

'What saddens me is the church's reaction; that you must have a nice genteel Gentile approach, nothing too public, you mustn't cause ripples etc. The "Jews for Jesus" approach is authentically Jewish culturally, and scratches where it itches. This is important, not only for "Jews for Jesus", but it is going to influence the whole pattern of Jewish evangelism in this country, not just by "Jews for Jesus", but by other missions as well. It is very important therefore that the different Jewish ministries stick together and work together very closely and don't allow the world and the church to divide them.'

The Holocaust is one of the things he has struggled with. It used to have an unhealthy fascination for him so that he found (and to some extent still finds) that he just wanted to watch or hear anything on television or radio about Germany from 1933 to 1945. Books on the Holocaust gripped him in quite an unhealthy way. It took him quite a while to work this through his system and become free in the Lord from it. He considers that the Holocaust must never be forgotten, but that there can be an unhealthy paranoia about it.

He has never felt that about Germany, to which he loves to go, and he preaches and lectures in Germany from time to time. Martin values his visits there almost more than to any other country, probably because of the German Jewish background of his family. He feels Jewish believers have something to say in Germany, in terms of the heart words of the Gospel–forgiveness, love, reconciliation, peace etc.

He remembers being at a Christian conference and talking with an older German elder in a Brethren assembly, and discovering that he had been in one of the camps, but on the 'other' side. After he was born again as a believer, he had nightmares that he was using his whip and driving thousands of naked Jews into the gas chambers. That memory still seared his conscience. Martin recalled with tears of joy how he was able to bring a word of forgiveness and peace into that man's troubled life. By his sacrificial death Jesus the Messiah cleanses us from all sin.

CHAPTER 12

A Remnant shall Return

HAVING SPENT SOME TIME in chapter 4 on the topic of God's covenant faithfulness, we now have to consider another biblical theme which is central to our identity as 'Messianic Jews', and that theme is 'the faithful remnant'. The description 'faithful' though commonly used, is not found in Scripture, and a better description would be 'remnant of grace'.

> But now, for a brief moment, the LORD our God has been gracious in leaving us a remnant and giving us a firm place in his sanctuary, and so our God gives light to our eyes and a little relief in our bondage (Ezra 9:8).

The biblical significance of the term is not just something that is left over, in the way that one might buy cheaply a remnant of material in a fabric department, what remains over when the rest has been used. In the biblical, technical sense a remnant is that through which, by reason of its existence, a whole group might escape the judgment of God (for example Abraham's prayer for Sodom, Gen 18:16ff.), or more usually through the history of Israel, a small group that guarantees the continuity of the nation when the bulk come under judgment.

> But God sent me ahead of you to preserve for you a remnant on earth and to save your lives by a great deliverance (Gen 45:7).
>
> Once more a remnant of the house of Judah will take root below and bear fruit above (2 Kings 19:30).
>
> What has happened to us is a result of our evil deeds and our great guilt, and yet, our God, you have punished us less than our sins have deserved and have given us a remnant like this (Ezra 9:13).

O Lord, God of Israel, you are righteous! We are left this day as a remnant. Here we are before you in our guilt, though because of it not one of us can stand in your presence (Ezra 9:15).

A remnant will return, a remnant of Jacob will return to the Mighty God (Is 10:21).

In that day the Lord Almighty will be a glorious crown, a beautiful wreath for the remnant of his people (Is 28:5).

Once more a remnant of the house of Judah will take root below and bear fruit above (Is 37:31).

I myself will gather the remnant of my flock out of all the countries where I have driven them and will bring them back to their pasture, where they will be fruitful and increase in number (Jer 23:3).

But one of the great fears was that one day God might leave Israel without a remnant, and that would be their end.

Shall we again break your commands and intermarry with the peoples who commit such detestable practices? Would you not be angry enough with us to destroy us, leaving us no remnant or survivor? (Ezra 9:14).

'Now this is what the Lord God Almighty, the God of Israel, says: Why bring such great disaster on yourselves by cutting off from Judah the men and women, the children and infants, and so leave yourselves without a remnant? (Jer 44:7).

While they were killing and I was left alone, I fell face down, crying out, 'Ah, Sovereign Lord! Are you going to destroy the entire remnant of Israel in this outpouring of your wrath on Jerusalem?' (Ezek 9:8).

This theme of the survival of Israel by reason of the survival of the remnant comes in over 50 places in the Old Testament, and is picked up by James in Acts 15:16,17 (quoting Amos 9:11,12) and by Paul in Romans 11:5, to show that those Jews who had come to faith in Jesus were fulfilling that remnant role.

After this I will return and rebuild David's fallen tent. Its ruins I will rebuild, and I will restore it, that the remnant of men may

seek the Lord, and all the Gentiles who bear my name, says the
Lord, who does these things (Acts 15:16-17).

So too, at the present time there is a remnant chosen by grace.
(Rom 11:5)

This is one reason why it is important that there are Messianic
Jewish congregations which continue to identify as an integral
part of the Jewish community. If, in expressing our faith in Jesus
as Messiah, and our oneness with our Gentile fellow members of
the body, we sever our connections with our fellow Jews, we
abdicate our calling to be the remnant by which Israel will
survive.

This theme of the solidarity between the remnant and the
larger group is a big issue, going beyond the theme of just Israel.
One example is the prayer of Abraham regarding God's impend-
ing judgement of Sodom, and asking God to spare the city for the
sake of the few righteous in it.

What if there are fifty righteous people in the city? Will you really
sweep it away and not spare the place for the sake of the fifty
righteous people in it? Far be it from you to do such a thing—to kill
the righteous with the wicked, treating the righteous and the
wicked alike. Far be it from you! Will not the Judge of all the earth
do right?' (Gen 18:24-25).

Another example is the account of the shipwreck in Acts 27,
where Paul is seen as the faithful remnant in that situation.

But now I urge you to keep up your courage, because not one of
you will be lost; only the ship will be destroyed. Last night an
angel of the God whose I am and whom I serve stood beside me
and said, 'Do not be afraid, Paul. You must stand trial before
Caesar; and God has graciously given you the lives of all who sail
with you.' So keep up your courage, men, for I have faith in God
that it will happen just as he told me. (Acts 27:22-25)

As long as the people stay with Paul, they are safe.

Then Paul said to the centurion and the soldiers, 'Unless these
men stay with the ship, you cannot be saved' (Acts 27:31).

It is not that their skills would be necessary for the final rescue: rather it is that safety was available only in the company of the remnant. In either case, whether the remnant stays with the group or the group stays with the remnant, the principle of solidarity is the same.

But perhaps the most telling example is after the Golden Calf incident, where God says he will destroy Israel and begin a new community with Moses and his children.

> 'I have seen these people,' the LORD said to Moses, 'and they are a stiff-necked people. Now leave me alone so that my anger may burn against them and that I may destroy them. Then I will make you into a great nation.' (Ex 32:9-10)

God's judgement is averted only by Moses' identification with the people as he intercedes for them.

> But now, please forgive their sin – but if not, then blot me out of the book you have written.' (Ex 32:32).

We recognise that this may sound arrogant to some, especially in the Jewish community, who see our very existence as a threat to their survival, rather than a cause for it. It may also sound like a claim of superiority within the body of Christ. We have to admit that in our immaturity we may actually sometimes give that impression. However the antidote is not to deny that place which we believe God has given us. If there is arrogance then we need to repent of it so that we might the more faithfully fulfil the role God has given us: the remnant is not without guilt.

> Who is a God like you, who pardons sin and forgives the transgression of the remnant of his inheritance? You do not stay angry forever but delight to show mercy (Mic 7:18).

> In those days, at that time, declares the LORD, search will be made for Israel's guilt, but there will be none, and for the sins of Judah, but none will be found, for I will forgive the remnant I spare (Jer 50:20).

In the sovereign mercy of God the remnant are not always the strong: they sometimes are the weak and the vulnerable.

I will make the lame a remnant, those driven away a strong nation. The LORD will rule over them in Mount Zion from that day and forever (Mic 4:7).

If this is something that, for the good of our own humility we Messianic Jews constantly have to remind ourselves of, then all disciples of Jesus, Jew and Gentile alike, need constantly to re-learn the same lesson.

But God chose the foolish things of the world to shame the wise; God chose the weak things of the world to shame the strong (1 Cor 1:27).

CHAPTER 13

I had come home.
Robert

I CAME TO FAITH in Jesus as the Messiah gradually over a period of several years between 1980 and 1983.

While I was growing up my parents belonged to the Reformed Synagogue in Edgware, but we were nominal members. We only went to 'shul' on the High Holy days, and that was with my father moaning, complaining and muttering and being dragged along by my mother. This attitude rubbed off on me: I didn't like going to Synagogue either.

We also went to Synagogue for Bar Mitzvahs and weddings, and that was about it. I did go to Cheder classes on a fairly irregular basis, but if I could find any sort of excuse I didn't go.

My mother's parents were slightly more religious than my father's. For example, they made Kiddush on a Friday evening, which my father's family didn't. So on quite a lot of Friday evenings we would go to my maternal grandparents and have Kiddush and a family meal with roast chicken and all the usual trimmings.

When I was about 17 or 18 I started getting interested in 'spiritual things' generally; meditation, Buddhism and other eastern religions, as well as Jewish and Christian mysticism. I decided to study comparative religion and went to Edinburgh University. I was really looking for something to live my life by, something more meaningful than just the materialistic middle class lifestyle of North London, which seemed fairly empty.

There were two or three committed Christians on the course with whom I had quite a lot of arguments about Christianity in general, about whether Jesus could be the Messiah, and even more fundamental things like whether there was a God or not. I also argued with them about why they didn't keep the Law if

Jesus said, 'Not a jot or a tittle shall pass away from the Law until all things come to pass'. Not that I was keeping the Law, but I thought they ought to be if they believed in Jesus.

There was no one particular thing that brought me to faith. I never did find an answer to the question of suffering, except that over a period of time I came to see that if Jesus was the Son of God, God hadn't stayed aloof, up in heaven, far away from our suffering. He had come down to earth and taken our sufferings on himself and suffered in exactly the way that we do, if not more so. That was really the thing that attracted me most to Jesus.

During this period I wasn't attending any place of worship. Every so often I would go along somewhere different. I went once to the Synagogue in Edinburgh on a Friday night; I went along to a Church of Scotland meeting and I went along to a Church of England service. Sometimes I went to an astrology group, encounter groups, and other such things.

When I came to faith there was no blinding flash of revelation. It was a gradual thing, though I can trace steps in it. At first it was very easy for me to accept that Jesus could have been a great Jewish prophet. Later I could accept that he might have been the Messiah as well, in the sense of the Messiah being just a human figure. There was a bigger hurdle in believing that he was the Son of God, in a way that no other human being was the Son of God. And even when I had eventually accepted that, it took me a long time before I felt that I wanted to, or even could, join a Christian congregation.

For a long time I enjoyed my faith on my own. I knew a couple of other Christians but I didn't go anywhere for worship. At the same time I maintained an interest in New Age philosophies. One Sunday, it was Pentecost, I went with a couple of friends to a little scenic valley, a river gorge, just outside Edinburgh, where we stayed for the weekend. There was a very beautiful renaissance chapel there which we went to on the Sunday morning. It was a completely dead service, so it seemed to me; but whenever I visited any services I always tried for myself to put meaning into those parts of the service in which I was participating. On this occasion it was as if there was a voice in my head which said, 'Don't you try and put any meaning into it; I'll put the meaning into it for you'. It became a very joyful service for me, even though the priest who was leading it seemed just to be going through the motions.

After that service I wanted to get baptised. Although I visited a couple of churches, there was none that I felt at home in until a friend suggested that I go along to the Catholic chaplaincy at the University. I really liked it. It was not the usual sort of Catholic Church building, but was run by the Dominican Brothers and they had part of the University premises, an old Georgian house in one of the squares.

The worship took place in a room on the first floor and all they had was a table with candlesticks at either end; no statues. There was one icon and that was the only decoration, apart from the altar table and the candlesticks.

I liked the service—a mass—and I particularly wanted to be able to take communion, but I knew enough about the Catholic Church to know that they wouldn't let me take communion unless I actually became baptised and a member of the Catholic Church. I went at least three times before I actually plucked up the courage to say to someone that I wanted to get baptised. The first person I mentioned it to looked at me in complete surprise and went off and grabbed the priest, the chaplain of the University, who asked me about my background and was completely shocked and dumbfounded when he found out that I was Jewish.

Eventually I started taking instruction. It did seem as though it was very much the right place for me, because the guy I was taking instruction from came from Manchester, and had grown up in an area where there had been quite a lot of orthodox Jews around. He knew about Jewish people and assured me that it wasn't a matter of me giving up being Jewish; it was the natural thing for Jews to be doing, to find the Jewish Messiah, and I wasn't to give up any of my Jewishness, but to bring it into and enrich the church.

So it was really a very good place for me to come into the church, for as he explained to me afterwards, he deliberately prolonged the period of instruction until I had an identity crisis halfway through it, because he was convinced that I would have doubts about what I was doing. He didn't actually try and bring them up, but he waited until they came up naturally, because he wanted them to come up before I was actually baptised, rather than afterwards.

One day, after I had spent weeks thinking 'Oh my God, what am I doing?' and 'Is Jesus really the Messiah?' and 'What's a Jewish guy like me doing getting into the Catholic Church?', I talked to the chaplain. He told me that though he thought my conviction was genuine, there was still something that I had to go through and resolve, and that I should pray about it. He didn't put any pressure on me and so I went away, really feeling better, having just talked about it. I prayed and thought through the situation further, and by the time I came back the next week my doubts were resolved. At the following Pentecost, in 1984, I was baptised, together with one other person.

I appreciate liturgical forms of worship. I think that's why I felt 'at home' in the Roman Catholic chaplaincy, and that in turn has developed my appreciation of liturgy. In liturgical worship you can concentrate on God rather than on what you are saying, because the words are so familiar and flow so easily. That gives a lot of depth to worship.

The other thing that attracted me was my desire to receive communion. I believed at the time and still do believe that communion–the bread and the wine–isn't just symbolic of Christ, and it isn't just a remembrance of Christ, but there is something in it that is spiritual food and drink to us, and that nourishes us. That was the main reason why I was attracted to Catholicism and is still something that I quite strongly believe.

When I came down to London I couldn't find a Catholic church that I felt at home in. I'm not very good at dealing with the statues, pictures and saints. I also disagreed with the way that communion was divorced from everyday life and kept inside the mass, whereas looking into the Bible I could see Christ saying that 'as often as you do these things you do it in remembrance of me.' I could see that in the context of Kiddush and the Passover meal etc, and didn't see why it could only be a priest who could administer communion. Beneath all this was my innate Jewishness, like a smouldering fire.

I first found out about the Messianic movement when I was in Edinburgh. Like a lot of Jewish believers, when I first became a believer, I thought I was the only one in the entire world. I remember reading a few books in the National Library of Scotland that looked at Jesus from a Jewish point of view. In one of them it mentioned the magazine of the Hebrew Christian Alliance. I asked for one of their magazines to be brought up to me in the reading room, got the HCA address, and wrote asking whether they had any services, in particular over Christmas, because I was going to be down in London for the Christmas period. They did not, but told me that the London Messianic congregation met in Finchley at St Luke's Hall every Friday at 8 o'clock. I phoned the man who was leading the congregation at that time, and he invited me to his flat, where I also met another Jewish believer. The feeling that I had mirrors the cliché that every Jewish believer talks about, I had come home in meeting two other Jewish believers.

CHAPTER 14

What is Judaism?
A Messianic Jewish Perspective

T HE CHURCH HAS BY AND LARGE not felt a need to understand how Jews have interpreted their own Scriptures, what it calls the 'Old Testament': it has developed its own methods of interpretation.

The Church has historically incorporated the Jewish Scriptures into its own Canon and developed its own methods of interpretation, without feeling the need to understand or grapple with Jewish methods of interpretation, or indeed with any of the developments within Judaism which are inextricably linked with those Scriptures. In more recent times, but mainly at the level of academic study, this is changing, though by and large it has not affected the way in which the Church expresses its faith.

Those Jews who have come to faith in Jesus as our Messiah, and who feel it right to continue to identify as Jews, and to live and worship in a Jewish way, cannot do that. We have to understand our new found faith from a Jewish viewpoint, both with regard to our Scriptures (and the context of the New Testament is in the main just as Jewish as the Old) and the rabbinic and other developments, if we are to be authentically Jewish. This does not mean that we uncritically accept and believe all these developments, but until we understand the richness of our inheritance, we shall not be able to make a mature judgment as to what we integrate and what we reject, and why.

Historically Christians have expressed at least an ambivalent attitude to things Jewish, and sometimes an openly hostile one. As regards the Torah (usually translated 'law' but better 'teaching') they have had a love-hate relationship. On the one hand they will rejoice that through Christ they have been set free from its bondage, and in the next breath they will sing with the psalmist 'Oh, how I love your law! I meditate on it all day long' (Ps 119:97).

In seeking to understand Judaism we have to begin with definitions. It may not seem the most interesting place to start, but in reality it is the only place. Definitions, in areas such as ours, meet serious problems. How objectively does the definition include those who rightly should be included and is yet able to exclude those who ought not to be in? In any case, who has the right to decide and to make definitions?

Who is a Jew? What is Judaism? Are these the same questions? We may feel that in general terms we know the answers, and if in detail we need help, then there will be somewhere that we can turn to where we can obtain a definitive answer. Or is there?

Some will want to begin by saying that Judaism is the religion based on what is called (in Christian circles at least) the Old Testament, and they will be surprised when the Jewish community, even the orthodox religious section within the community, finds great difficulty with that definition. Certainly the Jewish people look back to Abraham as their founder and father, they trace their ancestry to Abraham, through Jacob and Isaac. They look back to Moses as their great law-giver, they look back to the message of the prophets as being at the root of much of their ethical lifestyle, and the psalms are at the heart of their worship. But when we look more closely at the Judaism of today, indeed Judaism as it has developed over the past two and a half thousand years, and compare it with the Scriptures of the Tanach (the Jewish name for the Old Testament), we shall find discontinuity, indeed radical discontinuity, as well as continuity. If we want to understand Judaism today, not just cultural Judaism but Judaism as a living faith, we have to understand the reasons for that discontinuity.

In order to seek out the beginnings of Judaism (as distinct from what we might call Old Testament Religion) we shall need to undertake some word searches in the Scriptures, the outcome of which may well surprise us. We would be surprised that the word 'Israel' (and also Israelite, Israelites) features in over two thousand verses in the Old Testament and just eighty-one in the New Testament. We may be more surprised that the term 'Jew' and its related words occurs in just eighty-two verses in the Old

Testament, but in just over two hundred verses of the New Testament. There are more surprises in store. While 'Israel' etc are distributed fairly evenly through the period of the Old Testament, the word 'Jew' and its related terms do not occur historically before the middle period of Jeremiah's ministry. In other words, the beginnings of Jewish development are associated with the period of the Babylonian exile; thereafter, especially after the return from exile, the words Jew/Jewish become more common currency.

In both the Old and New Testaments, the terms 'Jew' etc are used more frequently of Jews in the Diaspora—the nations amongst whom the Jewish people have been scattered, either by enforced exile or by willing emigration—whereas 'Israelite' etc relates more to those living in the land of Israel. Further, 'Israelite' is used more frequently by Jews when referring to their own people, and 'Jew' used more frequently by Gentiles when referring to Jews.

This is seen most clearly in the parallel descriptions of events in the first three Gospels. In the birth and passion narratives, 'Israel' is used consistently in the context of Jewish speakers, whereas 'Jew' is the natural word on the lips of Gentiles, for example:

> 'But you, Bethlehem, in the land of Judah, are by no means least among the rulers of Judah; for out of you will come a ruler who will be the shepherd of my people *Israel*.' (Mt 2:6) (italics mine.)

compare

> After Jesus was born in Bethlehem in Judea, during the time of King Herod, Magi from the east came to Jerusalem and asked, 'Where is the one who has been born king of the Jews? We saw his star in the east and have come to worship him.' (Mt 2:1-2)

> 'He saved others,' they said, 'but he can't save himself! He's the King of *Israel*! Let him come down now from the cross, and we will believe in him.' (Mt 27:42) (italics mine.)

> Meanwhile Jesus stood before the governor, and the governor asked him, 'Are you the king of the *Jews*?' 'Yes , it is as you say,' Jesus replied. (Mt 27:11) (italics mine.)

This pattern runs throughout the first three Gospels, but is less clear in John's usage because of the variety of ways John uses the Greek word *Ioudaioi* to sometimes mean 'Jews', sometimes the 'Jewish leadership' or 'Judeans' (as distinct from Galileans).

If I have laboured the point, it has been to show that the situation is more complex than just equating Judaism with Old Testament religion. The reason this is important lies in the original context of the word 'Jew' in the exile. In Babylon, for the first time since their establishment as the Covenant People of God, the Children of Israel were unable to fulfil those command-ments of the Torah which were at the heart of the Covenant, namely those concerning offering of sacrifices. The very establish-ment of God's Covenants with his people used sacrificial termi-nology, in that a Covenant was not just 'made' it was 'cut' (Heb. *Karat*) indicating the involvement of the shedding of blood. Away from the Tabernacle, and later the Temple, sacrifice was not permitted; yet the whole basis of the maintenance of the relation between God and his Covenant People had depended on this.

> For the life of a creature is in the blood, and I have given it to you to make atonement for yourselves on the altar; it is the blood that makes atonement for one's life (Lev 17:11).

So new ways of relating to God, other than through animal sacrifices, had to be developed. We can perhaps begin to under-stand the magnitude of the religious revolution that faced the leaders of Israel as the nation went into captivity and exile; indeed so revolutionary were the changes that needed to be made, that a whole new class of leadership became necessary. In this way the new institution of the Synagogue was born, and the leaders of the period beginning with the Babylonian exile, such as Ezra, were later given the appellation of the 'Men of the Great Synagogue'.

Inevitably the priesthood became, to all intents and purposes, a redundant class, and in the place of sacrifice the other tenets of the faith of Israel came to the fore, namely new emphases on the Sabbath and those elements of the Torah which were not depend-ent on sacrifice, and developing new ways of celebrating the Festivals without sacrifice. Up to this point it was the emphasis on the holiness of God as expressed in the whole sacrificial Temple Liturgies which had separated the nation of Israel from the corrupt and often orgiastic practices of the worship of the surrounding nations. That is why the Temple and its worship were so closely guarded; why the offering of sacrifice at other places was so severely forbidden. For this kind of worship always degenerated into the practices of pagan worship as experienced in their 'high places'.

> I will destroy your high places, cut down your incense altars and pile your dead bodies on the lifeless forms of your idols, and I will abhor you (Lev 26:30).

> Even after this, Jeroboam did not change his evil ways, but once more appointed priests for the high places from all sorts of people. Anyone who wanted to become a priest he consecrated for the high places (1 Kings 13:33).

In all, dire warnings about worship on the 'high places' is given about sixty times in the Old Testament. However with the exile from Israel and the consequent loss of their Temple at Jerusalem, the temptation to the Jewish people to engage in this kind of worship must have been greatly heightened, and so the new leadership had to find ways of expressing the holiness of God and the separation of his Jewish People.

The basic principles of the Mosaic Law were expanded into a whole system of detailed observances as the new Teachers began to develop what became known as the Oral Tradition. In time the word 'Torah', primarily referring to the teaching of the five books of Moses, came to include that Oral Tradition also, and Jewish faith took on the belief that that Oral Tradition was actually given to Moses on Mount Sinai along with the Written Law. As such, it had the same validity and authority.

Thus, for example, while the Mosaic injunction was to keep the Sabbath holy, and do no work on it, the teaching of the Rabbis began to elucidate in great detail just what constituted forbidden work, and what was legitimate. As time went by this detail, called by the Rabbis a 'fence' around the law, evolved in ever increasing degrees of complexity.

It certainly succeeded in keeping the observant Jews separate from the peoples amongst whom they lived, but it also had the effect of bringing them into increasing bondage to the dictates of their leadership. It is vital that we understand the difference between Torah as the law given to Moses as we see it in Scripture and 'Torah' as Oral Tradition, which is the rabbinic interpretation and application. Jesus was totally loyal to the former,

> I tell you the truth, until heaven and earth disappear, not the smallest letter, not the least stroke of a pen, will by any means disappear from the Law until everything is accomplished (Mt 5:18)

but frequently engaged the rabbis in controversy over the latter. This distinction is so important that several examples will be quoted in full:

> Another time he went into the synagogue, and a man with a shrivelled hand was there. Some of them were looking for a reason to accuse Jesus, so they watched him closely to see if he would heal him on the Sabbath. Jesus said to the man with the shrivelled hand, 'Stand up in front of everyone.' Then Jesus asked them, 'Which is lawful on the Sabbath: to do good or to do evil, to save life or to kill?' But they remained silent (Mk 3:1-4).

> Woe to you, teachers of the law and Pharisees, you hypocrites! You give a tenth of your spices—mint, dill and cummin. But you have neglected the more important matters of the law—justice, mercy and faithfulness. You should have practised the latter, without neglecting the former (Mt 23:23).

> You have let go of the commands of God and are holding on to the traditions of men (Mk 7:8).

The Synagogue did not simply replace the Temple: it was a whole new concept. There had been only one Temple, that was of its essence. It had been the focal point of the worship of the one true God of Israel; it was the place of mediation and atonement by which sinful men and women could commune with the Holy God of Israel. All that had been swept away by the ruthless Babylonian invaders. A new way had to be found in which sacrificial atonement for sin was replaced by the desire to please God by observance of the Torah.

Each local Jewish community had its own synagogue which became the focal point of its corporate life, not just a place for worship but also a place of assembly, and most importantly of all, a place for teaching, a place of study of the Torah, with all its detailed rabbinic interpretations and applications. It is not without significance that still the most frequently used title for the synagogue is the 'shul'.

So great was the effectiveness of the new leadership that even after the return to the Land, the rebuilding of the Temple under Ezra and Nehemiah, and the re-establishment of sacrificial worship, the presence of the synagogue maintained an increasing influence, not only in Israel as a whole, but even in Jerusalem itself.

Let it be said that this increasing influence depended not just on the vitality of the new movement, but was assisted by an increasingly decadent lifestyle of the old priesthood and their frequent collaboration with the succession of occupying powers that invaded the land.

The new leaders, who became known as the Pharisees, were by contrast of the people, with the people, and above all, very patriotic. Despite Jesus' frequent clashes with the religious leadership of his day, including the Pharisees, biblical scholarship is showing increasingly the likelihood that Jesus himself lived as a Pharisee, and his controversy with them was not, as has been frequently portrayed, a blanket condemnation of all they stood for, but a criticism from within the movement of the 'bad eggs' in their midst.

By way of example the seven woes against the Pharisees, in Matthew 23 may well be a reflection of an already existing internal 'code of practice' in the pharisaic profession, which included a sevenfold condemnation of hypocritical Pharisees later present in the Talmud. Thus it was not criticism from outside the movement, but self regulation of discipline from within; the discipline that results from flagrant breaches of their own standards.

In the Tractate Sotah 22b of the Babylonian Talmud there is a section entitled 'The Plague of the Pharisees' (for brevity we summarise, and use also alternative explanations from the Jerusalem Talmud):

Our Rabbis taught: There are seven types of Pharisees: the Pharisee who carries his religious duties upon his shoulder osten-
tatiously. The Pharisee who walks with exaggerated humility. The
Pharisee who, in his anxiety to avoid looking upon a woman he
dashes his face against the wall. (The Jerusalem Talmud has a
very different rendering: a calculating Pharisee who performs a
good deed and then a bad deed, setting one off against the other.)
The Pharisee whose head is bowed like a pestle in a mortar. The
Pharisee who constantly exclaims 'What is my duty that I may
perform it?'—as though he had fulfilled every obligation. The
Pharisee from love, and The Pharisee from fear. Some Rabbis
interpret 'love' as denoting love of the rewards promised for the
fulfilment of precepts and 'fear' as fear of punishment for trans-
gressing them.[1]

All too soon after the Second (Herod's) Temple had been
completed and the sacrifices re-established, in CE 70, the Jewish
people had once more to face the trauma of their beloved Temple's destruction, and in CE 134, following an unsuccessful upris-
ing led by Simon Bar Kochba, the Roman armies razed
Jerusalem to the ground and rebuilt it as a Roman city named
Aelia Capitolina. All Jews were banned from even entering the
city and so began yet one more exile from the Land that was to
last until 1948.

Once again the Jews were without the Temple and therefore
without sacrifice, and again it was the responsibility of the Pharisees to continue in exile the work begun in Babylon by the Men
of the Great Synagogue, a work which culminated in the production of the Talmud (which was completed about 500 CE). This
was a massive work which, together with the Tanach (Old Testament) has been the foundational document for understanding
and interpreting Jewish Torah and spirituality ever since.

In one sense this was history repeating itself, with one main
difference; this time Judaism was seeing the greatest threat to its
survival not in the paganism of the nations that surrounded it and
invaded its land, but in the threats of a Christianity which was
claiming to be the true inheritor of the biblical covenants and
Israel's replacement as the People of God.

It is not our purpose here to note all the major developments
within Judaism over the past two thousand years, but as we are

focusing in this book on the birth and growth of Messianic Judaism there are two developments which we cannot ignore. First, the understanding of atonement, which is at the heart of the biblical revelation of God's relationship with mankind, created in his image and yet so far fallen from God's original purposes. Secondly, the development of thought relating to that person prefigured in the Tanach, the Lord's anointed, the Messiah. Hand in hand with this has naturally gone a development in the Jewish doctrine of man and of sin. Since a remedy for sin (ie. sacrifice) was no longer available, the diagnosis of the problem needed to be revised.

CHAPTER 15

The Truth Will Reveal Itself.
Ben

I GREW UP IN North West London. My father was born in Germany, into a very orthodox family. My mother was born in Africa and had a nominal Jewish upbringing. My father always tried to live an orthodox lifestyle, but was not encouraged by my mother to overdo it as she disliked the extremes of orthodoxy. As a child I could always sense a degree of disunity between my mother and father where religion was concerned.

I went to the Hasmonean Preparatory School and the Hasmonean Grammar School for Boys, which were orthodox Jewish schools. I found the religious people I knew very hypocritical when one compared their ritual of practising Judaism and what was really going on in their hearts and minds. As a result, I was put off religion, but nevertheless I still believed in God and that God was the truth. I always questioned the way one was obliged to keep things according to orthodox Jewish custom, compared with what was actually practised in the Bible, as there were often major differences between the two, so far as I could see it.

I always wondered why the second Temple had been destroyed and why we as a nation had been cast out into the Diaspora and why God should have rejected us for two thousand years. It was obvious we had sinned as a nation, but what was it we did that really provoked God to punish us for so long. Were we still committing the same sin?

I remember being taught by Rabbis at school that we do not live in an age of prophecy where the Holy Spirit would come upon people in dreams and visions and with gifts of healing. All these things no longer happened and even the Rabbis did not have sufficient authority from God, or a close enough relationship with him to have the confidence, say, to overrule Rabbis from earlier generations.

In my opinion, the religion had fossilised spiritually since the destruction of the second Temple. It was as if God was not working sufficiently in people's lives. They did not know what God wanted of them for today and they did not have this authority because the Holy Spirit had been removed.

The sole aim of orthodox Judaism seemed to me to be to try and preserve the status quo as rigidly as possible, in the hope that one day the Messiah would come, and Judaism would then become a living, flexible religion where all the gifts of the Holy Spirit as referred to in the Bible would be poured out upon the people, the Temple rebuilt, and all the exiles in the Diaspora would be restored to the land.

When I finished my 'A' levels I went to Yeshiva (a Talmudic College) in Jerusalem. I quite enjoyed studying Talmud and got a lot out of it. However, it was very legalistic. It did nothing to really alter my spiritual state, but only served my academic instincts. After going to Yeshiva, I did a law degree and then qualified as a solicitor.

In my late twenties I began to have real doubts about orthodoxy and I confronted the fact that I was not happy living the orthodox lifestyle. I actually said a prayer to God at that time along the lines of: 'Lord, I believe in your Bible, I believe in you, I believe in your Jewish people, I believe you have something special for your Jewish people, but somehow something just isn't right. I don't know what it is, but I do not believe that the way we practise Judaism today is how you want it done. I am not happy being orthodox and I want to give up, but it is not because I reject you, God.'

At that time, I lived in a flat which I wanted to redecorate and there were various builders who came round to quote. One of the builders struck me as being Jewish, so I asked him if he was. In reply he said 'Yes, I am a Messianic Jew'. I had never heard of the term Messianic Jew, so I asked him what it was. He explained that he believed that Jesus (Yeshua) was the Jewish Messiah. I listened to him and thought how this could be. I had never heard of Jews believing Jesus was the Messiah, and it was contrary to all the Jewish teaching I had received.

Nevertheless, he explained why he believed it and that it fitted his interpretation of the Hebrew Scriptures. I listened to him very intensely and saw something in him I had always expected to see in orthodox Jewish people, but had not seen before. He had a genuine spiritual sincerity and simplicity, and a knowledge and understanding of God, without any of the outward appearances of being religious. He just seemed godly; at least that is how it came across to me. Although I found it very hard to accept what he was saying, it prompted me to go away and look at my Scriptures and give the matter more thought.

Could Jesus really be the Messiah? The more I thought about it, I realised how incredible it would be if it were true; how it would confound everything I had been taught. I then started to read the New Testament for the first time in my life. What struck me most was that it was so Jewish and that the teachings and stories rang true. It made me wonder where the Gentiles got Catholicism and Protestantism from, and how they had managed to make Jesus seem so Gentile.

I realised that the New Testament was Jewish in origin and therefore a Jew could believe in it and claim it as his own. I did not feel that by believing in the New Testament I was doing anything other than believing in what other Jews had seen, believed and written about.

In essence, the picture I got from the New Testament was that the whole concept of forgiveness and the need for an atoning sacrifice, which is so central to Judaism, could only be obtained today through the blood of Messiah, through God's only Son, rather than the blood of bulls and goats, as there was no Temple.

The picture of Abraham on the verge of sacrificing his only son, and God stopping him, made me realise that Abraham must have understood and thought about the concept of resurrection. When he was going to sacrifice Isaac, he must have thought that God would resurrect Isaac, how else could God fulfil the promise that Abraham would be a father of many. I also believed that Isaac must have believed in resurrection, which is why he allowed himself to be bound and sacrificed. I realised that the imagery surrounding the sacrificing of one's only son was really so Jewish, and that God had not required it of Abraham and Isaac, but would require it of himself and his Son, the Messiah.

The story of Abraham and Isaac was clearly a forerunner of a greater story unfurled in the New Testament.

The concept of resurrection is manifest throughout the Jewish Scriptures, which are full of prophecies relating to the end times when the dead will be raised, when the Messiah will come to reign on earth and bring peace.

When I started to put the pieces of the jigsaw together (ie the New Testament and the Old Testament), it was incredible. In my heart I knew and believed that it was all true and as a result I found that my own relationship with God completely changed. For the first time in my life, I felt God's Holy Spirit in a dramatic way.

The irony is that when I became disillusioned with orthodox Judaism, I found myself turning away from my Jewishness. However, when I became Messianic my Jewishness was totally restored to me, but with a new understanding and with a new flavour and depth.

My first experience of going to a church was at the South Bank Fellowship in Richmond. I was very reluctant to go and felt very uncomfortable indeed. I even rolled up three quarters of the way through the service so that I would not have to suffer it for too long. I walked in and sat at the back with the intention of just being an observer. However, it did not take very long before I was genuinely choked and touched by the fact that some people were on their knees being humble before God, some held their hands lifted up to God in worship, and the songs and music were so appropriate and meaningful. It was a very charismatic, casual house church service; very unlike anything I had ever seen either on television or in films, where the church was portrayed as very cold, dead and staid.

As I watched from the back, I realised that I had never seen people cry in synagogue, nor had I ever experienced such sensitivity in worship, yet here were Gentiles worshipping God in a way that I always thought they would be incapable of, as supposedly only Jews could really worship God properly. I realise this ignorance was in part due to my narrow orthodox upbringing. I was filled with jealousy that the Gentiles could have such beautiful fellowship, and worship God in spirit and in truth in this way, when all we had was rigid, liturgical prayers with very

little room for any free worship. Our services seemed so boring
and dead in comparison.

It struck me that maybe the Gentiles did have the Holy Spirit
(as I really sensed the presence of God at that service) and maybe
the Jews had lost it. This did have a dramatic effect on me and for
a long while I refused to go to a church service again. Nevertheless, I did slowly learn that the Gentiles also needed to have a
relationship with God, that God had made them and loved them,
and that they too could be godly.

I also discovered a new approach to walking with God where
the emphasis was on what was going on in your heart, mind and
soul, rather than what you expressed on the outside. It was not
about wearing your religion on the surface or practising an external ritual of prayer.

I could also see that there was a much more genuine interac-
tion between other believers from the way that they prayed
together and for each other, whether on an individual basis, or as
a group, or just among friends, and that they really involved God
in all aspects of their lives. They had a different kind of relationship with God and it really appealed to me and I found it very
refreshing. I had no problem accepting it and feeling very comfortable with it. As a result, I made very good Gentile friends for
the first time in my life.

I believe, just as God moved Moses out of Egypt from Phar-
aoh's household, to live with the Midianite people and eventually
marry a Midianite woman, so God moved me out of my very
narrow and blinkered North West London orthodox background
into a godly Gentile community where he could open my eyes to
see that he wanted to reach out to the Gentiles just as much as he
wanted to reach out to the Jews.

There are so many passages in the Bible where God talks
about his Temple being a place of prayer for all nations and that
the Jewish nation is called to be a light to the Gentiles. Right from
the beginning I believe God wanted the Gentiles to come in and
be part of his overall plan for salvation. Yet, when I look at
orthodox Jews, they seem to be so cut off from society at large.
They do not even mix with irreligious Jews, never mind Gentiles.
So how can God use them to be this light? I do feel God has

widened my perspective and understanding enormously in this respect and I am very grateful for it.

From the day when I had my first conversation with the decorator who came to give me a quote to decorate my flat, I shared with my family what had happened, and as I progressed in my understanding of Messianic Judaism, I continued to share it with them. Most people around me found it quite interesting, but I do not think they fully understood at the outset that it was a real walk of faith. When it became clear that I was really committed, I did have some problems with them, but I found that quite easy to deal with.

Primarily, most people feared that I had deserted the Jewish faith, but I thought that was a shallow argument, as it simply was not true. I kept the Jewish Sabbath and all the Jewish festivals. I prayed to the same Jewish God I had always prayed to previously. I always made it clear that I believed Yeshua was not a man who had become God, but instead God who had become fully man. I also showed them passages in the Jewish Scriptures that made clear references to the Messiah, that said a son would be born and called 'Wonderful Counsellor, Mighty God, Everlasting Father, Prince of Peace' and the people would bow down and worship him as part of the Godhead.

Between members of my family there has always been a lot of teasing on the subject of religion, and although they may question what I believe in, I equally question the things they believe in. On the whole, we have a good and healthy understanding. The most important thing to me is that my family does recognise that I have a very strong faith and relationship with God and they do respect me for it and see that it is genuine.

Even though I have made Gentile friends, it is still very important for me to have Jewish friends who are believers and, therefore, I have always committed myself to attending a Messianic congregation to worship on the Jewish Sabbath and Festivals.

For the future, I hope that the Messianic movement will grow and mature into a full community of believers with school, synagogues, youth clubs, cemeteries etc. I hope it always maintains its Jewishness, so that the Jewish community at large can see clearly that in all respects we keep and believe the same things as they do, save in respect of the Messiahship of Yeshua.

Although the famous Rabbi Akiva wrongly believed that Bar Kosibah, renamed Bar Kochbah, was the Messiah and the Lubuvitch movement wrongly believes Rabbi Shnearson will be proclaimed the Messiah, no one would say they are no longer Jews. Similarly, I hope Messianic Jews will still be treated and seen as Jews by the community at large, even though the majority of Jews may think we've got it wrong. The truth is, it is impossible to prove that even God exists let alone that Jesus is the Jewish Messiah, and at the end of the day it all boils down to one's personal faith and beliefs. The truth will only reveal itself when Messiah actually comes.

CHAPTER 16

Atonement? Who Needs It?

F ROM THE POINT OF VIEW of the Jewish Scriptures alone, the human race, though originally created in the image of God, is a fallen race. 'The LORD was grieved that he had made man' (Gen 6:6); 'the heart of man is deceitful above all things' (Jer 17:9); 'there is no-one who does good, not even one' (Ps 14:3). These are not isolated 'proof texts', but part of a consistent theme that runs through the Scriptures regarding the fallen nature of mankind. Indeed the magnitude of the problem was reflected in the radical nature of the remedy: vicarious life sacrifice.

> For the life of a creature is in the blood, and I have given it to you to make atonement for yourselves on the altar; it is the blood that makes atonement for one's life (Lev 17:11).

Yet nowadays an orthodox Rabbi, Yechiel Eckstein, can write:

> Man is intrinsically pure since he was created by God, the embodiment of absolute purity and goodness.... This Jewish view of the nature of humankind stands in sharp contrast with the classical Christian one that suggests that as a result of Adam's sin, all future generations of man become tainted with Original Sin. In the Jewish view, sin is a human action, not a condition. In the dominant Christian view, however, man is so caught up in his sinfulness that he lacks the ability for self regeneration.[1]

It is telling that this concept of 'self regeneration' recurs frequently in Jewish spirituality. For example, in Talmudic teaching about the 'new heart' the emphasis is on such verses as Ezekiel 18:31.

> Rid yourselves of all the offences you have committed, and get a new heart and a new spirit. Why will you die, O house of Israel?

This is interpreted as a command from God which his people can fulfil by their own efforts.

> I will give you a new heart and put a new spirit in you; I will remove from you your heart of stone and give you a heart of flesh (Ezek 36:26)

Such passages as the above, where the emphasis is on God's sovereign initiative, are interpreted by the Rabbis as exceptional and extreme cases where the people had gone so far from God that only his initiative can bring them back.

In a similar vein, in a recent Haggadah (Passover liturgy) prepared by a group of orthodox American rabbis we read:

> Passing through the waters
>   amidst signs and wonders
>   was this our people born!
> Out of the fiery furnace,
>   seared in body and soul,
>   reborn in self redemption,
> Finding favour in the wilderness,
> The people Israel lives![2]

Eckstein continues by quoting Rabbi Abraham Heschel:

Christianity starts with one idea about man; Judaism with another. The idea that Judaism starts with is that man is created in the likeness of God. You do not have to go far, according to Judaism, to discover that it is possible to bring forth the divine within you and the divine in other men.... It is with that opportunity that I begin as a Jew. Christianity begins with the basic assumption that man is essentially depraved and sinful—that left to himself he can do nothing. He has to be saved.... The first question of Christianity is: 'What do you do for the salvation of

your soul?' *I have never thought of salvation. It is not a Jewish problem*
(italics mine).[3]

We see here, as in much Jewish writing, a fundamental misunderstanding of the Christian doctrine of total depravity and salvation by faith. Even allowing for that, we see a watering down of
the biblical teaching of the fallenness of man and the need for an
objective, God-given atonement. For the Rabbis the problem is
not so big that only God can solve it; man has within himself all
that is needful.

Jewish theologians are not blind to human sinfulness; after all,
after the Shoah how could they be? Rabbinic Judaism teaches
that within man reside two inclinations, a good and a bad, a
yetzer ha-tov and a yetzer ha-ra. But these are only 'inclinations';
they can be resisted and channelled in the power of the human
spirit. And even the yetzer ha-ra, the evil inclination, is not
absolutely evil. It can be described as man's inner drive, the drive
to get on, the drive to survive, the drive to procreate. Were it not
for the yetzer ha-ra, remarks a rabbinic Midrash on Genesis 7:9,
'a man would not build a house, or marry, or have children, or
engage in commerce.'[4]

In a similar vein is a legend in the Talmud (Yoma 69b) that
the men of the Great Synagogue wanted to kill the yetzer ha-ra,
who warned them that if they were successful the 'world would go
down', ie come to an end. They therefore imprisoned him (ie the
yetzer) for three days and then searched the land for a new laid
egg without finding one[5] (ie all the hens had lost their reproduc-
tive capacity).

To summarise, the evil inclination is that in man which relates
to the practicalities of living out his humanity, whilst the good
inclination has to do with man's spiritual dimension, his relationship with God, though in Judaism this dichotomy is much less
evident than it is in much traditional Christianity. Evil is seen as
using what is God given in ways that are man-centred, self-
centred, rather than God-centred. The important thing to understand is that the evil inclination need not be, in New Testament
terms, 'put to death', 'put off', 'crucified'; *indeed it must not be*. Rather
it needs to be channelled and directed in the service of God.

The Jewish view of the physical world is that it too is intrinsically good. Man has the privilege and, indeed the obligation to derive pleasure from it and to avail himself of its goodness. These are points that Christians need to hear, but for the moment we shall concentrate on the nature of the Jewish view of the fallenness of the created order, and its remedy, and see how far they have developed from their biblical beginnings.

Regarding biblical teaching on sacrifice, Rabbi Moses Maimonides, the leading 12th century Jewish theologian, taught that the sacrificial system was not of Jewish origin, but that it was the universal custom among all peoples at the time of Moses to worship by means of sacrifices. His view was that since the Israelites had been brought up in this atmosphere, God realised that they could not immediately abandon sacrifice. He therefore limited its application by confining it to one place in the world, with the ultimate intention of weaning them from the debased religious rituals of their idolatrous neighbours.

This is not to suggest that Maimonides was saying anything very revolutionary or new, as far as Jewish thinking was concerned, though he did bring into sharp focus the almost inevitable conclusion of the way Jewish thinking was going. Already it was being said that Torah observance was replacing sacrifice, this teaching being based on such texts as 1 Samuel 15:22.

> But Samuel replied: 'Does the LORD delight in burnt offerings and sacrifices as much as in obeying the voice of the LORD? To obey is better than sacrifice, and to heed is better than the fat of rams'.

> You do not delight in sacrifice, or I would bring it; you do not take pleasure in burnt offerings (Ps 51:16).

> With what shall I come before the LORD and bow down before the exalted God? Shall I come before him with burnt offerings, with calves a year old? Will the LORD be pleased with thousands of rams, with ten thousand rivers of oil? Shall I offer my firstborn for my transgression, the fruit of my body for the sin of my soul? He has showed you, O man, what is good. And what does the LORD require of you? To act justly and to love mercy and to walk humbly with your God (Mic 6:6-8).

Rabbinic Judaism has moved away from that sacrifice-centred view which we believe to be at the heart of biblical teaching.

Nevertheless orthodox Judaism, while on the one hand sees the Temple sacrifices as no longer relevant and necessary, still looks forward to the rebuilding of the Temple and the reinstitution of the sacrifices during the Messianic era. The 'Amidah' prayer of the Siddur concludes

> that the Temple may be speedily rebuilt in our days...And there we will serve Thee with awe...Then shall the offering of Judah and Jerusalem be pleasant unto the Lord, as in days of old, and as in ancient years.[6]

The position of Jewish orthodoxy is well stated by Michael Friedlander:

> The revival of sacrificial service must...be sanctioned by the divine voice of a prophet. The mere acquisition of the Temple mount by Jews...could not justify the revival. It is only the return of the Jews to Palestine, and the rebuilding of the Temple by divine command and divine intervention, that will be followed by the restoration of the sacrificial service.[7]

This tension within Orthodox Judaism has not been satisfactorily resolved, and the Reform and Liberal movements within Judaism have so reformed the liturgy that it no longer anticipates the restoration of Temple or sacrifice, viewing any objective doctrine of atonement of this nature as part of a primitive religion discarded a long time ago by modern man come of age.

We can understand why, in the inevitable absence of sacrificial atonement in Judaism since CE 70, the biblical doctrine of sin has had to be toned down. Is this consistent with the teaching of the Talmud, however?

> Why are idolaters lustful? Because they did not stand at Mount Sinai. For when the serpent came upon Eve he injected lust into her: [as for] the Israelites who stood at Mount Sinai, their lustfulness departed; the idolaters, who did not stand at Mount Sinai, their lustfulness did not depart (Shabbat 145b–146a)[8]

What this is saying is that following Eve's fall depravity did enter into the human race, but Israel, by taking upon itself the yoke of the Torah, was delivered from it ('idolaters' in this context is to be understood as Gentiles). However the footnote of the Soncino edition of the Talmud explains that 'those who accept the moral teaching of the Torah (implying not only Jews) are freed.'[9]

This 're-interpretation' of Talmud releases Gentile Christians from the traditional charge of idolatry. Rabbi Sylvia Rothschild, in the Easter Sunday 1991 'Heart of the Matter' television programme, explained that for a Christian to believe in the divinity of Jesus was not idolatry, but for a Messianic Jew so to believe clearly was! However Rabbi Dr Dan Cohn-Sherbok, a Visiting Professor at the University of Essex, in an article entitled *Why Today's Society needs to reconsider the forgotten Doctrine of Original Sin*, writes:

> The rabbis taught that death was the result of Adam's disobedience; they did not teach a doctrine of original sin. Nonetheless, they believed that the wickedness of man was great in the earth, and that every imagination of the thoughts of his heart was only evil continually (Gen 6:5).

They explained this condition by positing the existence of the evil inclination.

Dr Cohn-Sherbok continues:

> Drawing on this tradition Paul taught that sin came into the world through Adam and one man's trespass led to the condemnation of all men (Rom 5:18).

He then traces this line of thought through Augustine and the Protestant reformers – 'they stressed the complete depravity of human beings' – and concludes:

> In the modern world this Judeo-Christian understanding of inherent human evil has largely been lost.[10]

In favourably quoting Paul in Romans 5:18, it is noticeable that Dr Cohn-Sherbok is not willing to accept the full context of that verse, which makes two vital points:

> Therefore, just as sin entered the world through one man, and

death through sin, and in this way death came to all men, because all sinned—for before the law was given, sin was in the world. But sin is not taken into account when there is no law. Nevertheless, death reigned from the time of Adam to the time of Moses, even over those who did not sin by breaking a command, as did Adam, who was a pattern of the one to come. But the gift is not like the trespass. *For if the many died by the trespass of the one man,* how much more did God's grace and the gift that came by the grace of the one man, Jesus Christ, overflow to the many! Again, the gift of God is not like the result of the one man's sin: The judgment followed one sin and brought condemnation, but the gift followed many trespasses and brought justification. For if, by the trespass of the one man, death reigned through that one man, how much more will those who receive God's abundant provision of grace and of the gift of righteousness reign in life through the one man, Jesus Christ. Consequently, just as the result of one trespass was condemnation for all men, so also the result of one act of righteousness was justification that brings life for all men. *For just as through the disobedience of the one man the many were made sinners, so also through the obedience of the one man the many will be made righteous.* The law was added so that the trespass might increase. But where sin increased, grace increased all the more, so that, just as sin reigned in death, so also grace might reign through righteousness to bring eternal life through Jesus Christ our Lord (Rom 5:12-21).

1. Torah, far from bringing deliverance from the effects of Adam's transgression, was given in order to highlight it (v 20).

2. What the Torah is unable to achieve has been achieved by Jesus

so also the result of one act of righteousness was justification that brings life for all men (Rom 5:18b).

If the rabbinic leadership of current Judaism is willing to reconsider this teaching, it should naturally lead to a reconsideration of the Jewish understanding of the nature and role of the Messiah. This will be the theme of chapter 18.

Where there are Jewish leaders who are so open to reconsidering at least some points of New Testament teaching which they have until now rejected, there is encouragement for Jewish believers in Jesus to continue to identify as Jews.

CHAPTER 17

This Man is Searching for You.
Ralph

I WAS BORN IN Khartoum, Sudan in 1945, into an Orthodox Jewish family of complex background. On my mother's side the family can be traced back to Spain at the time of the Inquisition, and then on to Tiberias, from where my grandfather, a Rabbi, was invited to become the Chief Rabbi of the Sephardi Jewish community in Sudan. Under his leadership the community thrived and grew to a membership of about three hundred.

My father's family background has German and Romanian origins, his grandfather having been a Rabbi in Romania: so I have Rabbis in my family background on both sides.

My father came from Cairo, and moved to Sudan in order to open an optical practice in Khartoum. Our family was large, there having been twelve children on my mother's side, and I had forty cousins! We were all brought up within the close knit structure of Orthodox Jewish life, with the grandmother of the family keeping us all together. Life was rich and full, with all that the festivals and the fun that such a Jewish life had to offer.

I had my Bar Mitzvah at the age of thirteen, and entered into the keeping of our faith as fully as I could, putting on my tallit (prayer shawl) and tephillin (phylacteries) daily for prayer. It was a very special time for me. At this time, despite the outward family closeness, my parents divorced, which was a tremendously painful time, and my faith and prayer-life were the means of finding the peace and identity I was searching for. My mother went to America and I remained with my father, until at the age of seventeen I came to England to study for A levels at Wittinghame College in Brighton, and then Ophthalmic Optics at the City University in London.

This was the first time that I met Liberal Jews, who didn't live their Jewish lifestyle, or observe the festivals as rigorously as we had. For the first time I found myself in the position of having to think through these issues, and gradually I moved away from my Orthodox practices.

While studying Ophthalmic Optics I met Helen doing the same course, and, in a manner of speaking, we looked into each other's eyes and fell in love.

Although by now I had dropped a lot of my Jewish practice, I maintained observance of Yom Kippur, the Day of Atonement, because I felt that somehow, by suffering, one was nearer God.

Helen was a nominal Christian. As I wanted the blessing of a 'holy man', and Helen also felt that a religious ceremony was important, we married in St Anne's Church, Bagshot, where the vicar was excellent. Some of the things he said reminded me of my grandfather, such as 'find the truth, and lock it in your heart'. Neither Helen nor I 'converted', and in the service I didn't have to say anything I didn't believe, which was important to me. Early on we adopted our eldest son, Mark, because we had been told we might not be able to have children, but then we had two of our own, James and Oliver.

After the children came, I was very involved with making money. Money was my god at the time. I was an Ophthalmic Optician in Highcliffe for one year, and then we moved to Ferndown where we lived for 18 or 19 years. I started off working for a company and then went into partnership with Mr Hatfield, a lovely Christian man who proved his Christian faith in his life. He was a Methodist preacher and his example, and especially his wife's, was a real blessing to me. I will always remember his wife dying of liver cancer, and yet she was a witness to the Lord up to the end, and that spoke to me later on.

We entered a partnership and then we started a practice at home which Helen ran, which produced many amusing incidents. Then a health centre opened and we were invited to move the practice there. We did quite a bit of research in the practice which is well documented, including the Duochrome Technique. I became secretary and chairman of the local optical committees and president of the Orthoptics Association. In a lot of ways I felt I had made it in the world. In my profession I had reached the peak; invited to go on a number of committees, and did research within the practice on glaucoma, and we were asked to liaise with the diabetic clinic, following which I was involved in writing one section of a book about diabetes.

Professionally and financially we had made it. We had a wonderfully big house with everything you can imagine, seven bedrooms, indoor swimming pool and tennis court; in human terms I was there. But there was a void within me, a hunger for something that God had for me throughout that time. We met some friends through the Round Table. Clive kept inviting Helen and me to different things, and Sue as a hairdresser ended up cutting my hair. So I was being witnessed to while I was having my hair cut! They belonged to St John's Church, Wimborne, and apparently had prayer triplets who prayed for us.

Suddenly, one evening, I felt I needed to know more about this Jesus. I went to see a local vicar, Rev Christopher Blissard-Barnes, and simply said 'I am a Jew who wants to know about Jesus'. We talked, he gave me three books, *Basic Christianity*, *Journey Into Life*, and *The Way Ahead*. He suggested that I read the New Testament, and arranged to come and visit me.

A week after I saw him, Helen was at the early morning service at St Mary's. Christopher was talking about Jesus standing at the door, and the need to open the door into our life, and she suddenly realised that she had never done that. She opened the door then, and the Spirit moved her to tears. Christopher wondered what was happening to her. We feel very greatly blessed that the Lord brought us together to him at the right time. I always feel sad for couples where only one has come to the Lord.

Two weeks later Christopher came to our house and asked me again if I had read the New Testament, and I said I hadn't. Then he went on to share that there were four Gospels and that one was written by a doctor, which I might be interested in reading. He recognised I was obviously searching and asked if he could pray for me. I thought, being a good Jewish boy, there is nothing wrong in that, and he could pray for me. I imagined he would bring out a Prayer Book and read from it. But he did something very unusual; he put his hands together and although I can't remember his exact words he simply said, 'God, this man is searching for you; will you reveal yourself to him'. Then he went, and I remember thinking at the time, and saying to Helen, that it was like a telephone; he really believed that he could talk to God so directly. I thought, if that is how to reach God I am going to read the New Testament and discover more about him.

So I read the Gospels, and it was as though my grandfather was talking, and it spoke to my heart. One passage in particular spoke to me, when Jesus appeared to the disciples and said 'Peace be with you', and then later on 'May the peace of the Lord be with you'. I thought at the time, of course, he would greet his disciples with the Jewish greeting 'Shalom aleichem'. I am sure if God appears now he would simply say 'Good morning'.

I felt very at home reading the New Testament, it was so very Jewish. It was really the truth coming alive. But I reached a point where I said, okay, Jesus could be the Messiah (and I know what that means to a Jew—it is a big thing to swallow), and I could believe he did come 2,000 years ago, and it says that he is going to come some time in the future, but to me it is important to know that Jesus is alive today—not that he came in the past, or that he is coming in the future. I wanted someone to come and say to me that Jesus was alive today. In fact I thought I wanted half a dozen, but I would have been happy if just one person said it.

The next day, after a restless night, I woke up with a desire to go to church. I told Helen that I was going to church with her. There was a new curate, Rev Bill Salmon, at the church, and it was his first morning. He was one of those guitar-singing curates, and I always remember him standing up and apologising for not using Ancient and Modern, and for using the overhead projector to teach a new song. It was 'Jesus is alive today'. That was mind-blowing. I had just asked for it. People can argue coincidences but I would still say that it was God's perfect timing. That was the first step in a lot of questioning, with Christopher and Bill having to give me answers as I read through the New Testament. But it was the start of the journey where Jesus became my Messiah, my Saviour.

Time passed as I grew in my new found faith and entered into greater involvement in the life of the church. Eventually I felt a call to ordination over a period of years. In 1987 I went to a Vocation Conference at Trinity to test the call. I returned, certain of the call, but not sure whether it would be Non-Stipendiary

Ministry or full-time. I had however concluded that if it was to be NSM I could study at Salisbury and keep the practice, but if it was to be full-time, I would study at Bristol, and we would have to sell everything and leave it all behind.

Helen had a picture of the 'Start-rite' advert with the boy carrying a satchel and the girl walking beside him; they come to a crossroads; one way to Salisbury and the other to Bristol. Jesus was at the crossroads, and they asked him which way. He said, 'you choose'; the way to Salisbury was well lit, you could see exactly where you were going. But the other way was very dark and you couldn't really see where you were going, but the boy had to leave his satchel behind and Jesus walked between the boy and girl holding their hands. I prayed for a long time and then told Helen that it was to be full-time, holding Jesus' hand. So we sold our house and the practice, and here I am, an Anglican priest.

Going back to college was quite a painful time; the spiritual part of having to start at the bottom of a ladder when I had been at the top of something else. It was a difficult time in many ways, and before I left college I really wasn't certain whether I was doing the right thing. I wrote to my tutor saying I was seriously considering not going forward with the ministry.

At this time I went with a college mission team to St Mary's, Longfleet. Following the meeting of the housegroup I was asked to lead, I suggested that we pray for each other. There was specific prayer for a variety of people and situations, but no one prayed for me and I sat there thinking, 'if they only knew how I felt they would say something', but they didn't.

Afterwards, over coffee, I mumbled 'Can I have prayers for when I lead the Thursday service in the mission', and Ray, one of the local leaders, stood up and said, 'No, but we must all lay hands on you because God has something to say to you'. The prophetic message was in Arabic. Ray did not speak Arabic and so I could not believe it; he thought he was speaking in tongues! What he said was, 'My beloved son, I have called you, you are from the blood, the line of Abraham, I have called you into ministry. The Lord loves you'. And in English, he added 'You are to proclaim the Gospel and bring my people to the kingdom'. By then I felt absolutely drained: to think that God would want to speak to me in the language I was brought up in!

There was total silence for a few minutes and then Pam, Ray's wife, said these Gospel words which were in her mind, 'The battle is not yours but mine', and added 'You are not to doubt your ministry; minister in my name and proclaim the Gospel'. Ray added he had some words but was concerned they might be too painful 'Breathe in his love, strength and courage. Do not be afraid, I am with you always. Many will be brought into the kingdom by you. Go and proclaim the Gospel and minister in my name'. I shared my doubt with them, about the ministry and how much the words were confirmation that I should enter the ministry, and another person added that he felt he should say to me that I should be ordained that summer, but he didn't know what it meant. To this day I still wonder why God should produce this miracle just for me. I remember coming back, and the first thing Helen said to me was that my tutor had phoned wanting to speak to me about my letter. I phoned him and said forget it!

Early on I had preconceived ideas that Goyim (non-Jews) are there to get rid of us Jews in some way or another. I still believe the church is very Gentile, and I am saddened to see churches and Christians being so building-based rather than home-based. We have lost something from the Jewish tradition of things happening in the home, and I can't think of many Christian families who, after a Sunday service, will go home and share a prayer time and break bread and wine as they would do in a Jewish home. We need to go back to our roots and rediscover that something special which we have lost. Because of that, we have lost our ability to share our faith with our families and our children. I am very excited that our boys have grown up in a Christian home and they can share in that.

I am sad that the land that our Lord Jesus walked on has got so much bloodshed and pain. I pray that the Jews will be seen in a new light and so will their Arab neighbours. I pray that the Christians who are there, especially the Messianic believers, will be a bridge to join them up. The land of Israel is deep in God's heart and Jesus cried for Jerusalem. I am sure the Lord cries every time he sees Israel, the state it is in, and we need to cry with him in our prayers.

CHAPTER 18

A Messiah for God's People

A T THE CENTRE OF the divide between Judaism and Christianity is the figure of Jesus. Is he the Messiah? What are Jewish Messianic beliefs and expectations, and on what are they based?

The Jewish understanding of the Messiah is also crucial for the self understanding of Messianic Jews. Not that we regard rabbinic interpretations as having authority in matters of faith; we see God's revelation in matters of faith as vested in the Tanach and the Brit Hadashah, the Scriptures of the Old and New Covenants. However it is important that if we want our claim to the title 'Messianic Jews' to carry any integrity, both for ourselves and in our witness to the Jewish community, then we must seek to establish that there are valid Jewish reasons for our understanding of who Yeshua is.

It will become clear that there are fundamental differences between our understanding and current rabbinic understanding of the person and work of the Messiah. But has this always been so? Is current rabbinic thinking in line with that of those ancient rabbis who are so greatly venerated? How great is the variety of views held in Judaism over the centuries? Have there been views expressed about which it can be said, 'If these have been accepted within the broad sweep of Jewish belief, then it cannot be said that we are un-Jewish'. These are the areas we shall concentrate on in this chapter.

The twelfth of the 'Thirteen Principles of Faith' in the Siddur, the Jewish Prayer Book, reads:

> I believe with perfect faith in the coming of the Messiah, and, though he tarry, I wait daily for his coming.[1]

In that sense, therefore, Orthodox Jews would themselves claim to be Messianic Jews, and resent those who follow Jesus as Messiah and take this title for themselves. We need to ask therefore 'Just what is the Jewish understanding of things Messianic?' The question is simple to ask but complex in its answer.

THE JEWISH UNDERSTANDING OF THE MESSIAH

The Hebrew root is MSCH from which we get Mashiach (Messiah) the anointed one. Most frequently the word is used in its verbal form, 'to anoint', and is used most often for the anointing for offices of priests, kings and prophets. Objects for sacred use, eg the altar, were also anointed. In all, the word in its various forms, is used over seventy times in the Old Testament.

In its general application it has to do with the setting aside of ordinary human beings, and sometimes inanimate objects, for special tasks in the purposes of God. Nevertheless, in Scripture there is a line of development which sees a coming Messianic figure, whose description goes beyond that of an ordinary human being, even beyond that of a human king. There has also grown up in the Jewish consciousness, and in the teachings of its leadership, a firm belief that a 'deliverer' will come to bring great blessings from God, and the person who will bring these blessings is called the Messiah.

Shmuel Arkush, on television, portrayed the person and work of the Messiah as seen in Orthodox Judaism in this way:

> The Messiah will be somebody who will rebuild the third Temple, he is somebody who will ingather the exiled Jewish people, he will be somebody who will bring peace to the Jewish people and through them to the whole world. These are the three major jobs of the Messiah; and this is what the Jewish people are awaiting as their Messiah. Christianity has taken our patented invention, the Messiah, our man, and elevated him to great heights of being the Son of God, which from a Jewish point of view is unnecessary, and not only unnecessary, but in fact it excludes him from being the Messiah. These three jobs are still waiting to be done.[2]

On the same programme, Sylvia Rothschild, presenting the view of Liberal Judaism, covered much the same points, but prefaced her remarks with 'a Jewish Messiah anyway is a very vague idea,' and concluded:

> The Messiah for Christians, as I understand it, is that he has to be divine. He is, if you like, man's God whereas the Jewish Messiah would be God's man. And the split is in that sense theologically total.[3]

The Jewish Encyclopaedia states that the figure of Messiah, who would be raised up by God to break the yoke of the heathen and reign over a restored kingdom of Israel, is a strictly post biblical (ie post Old Testament) concept.

> The title 'Messiah' as a designation of the eschatological personality does not exist in the Old Testament; it occurs only from the time of the Second Temple after the Old Testament period.... In rabbinic thought, the Messiah is the king who will redeem and rule Israel at the climax of human history and the instrument by which the kingdom of God will be established.[4]

On the other hand in reform and liberal Judaism, belief in a personal Messiah is replaced by belief in a messianic age.

> The principles regarding the Messiah in the Reform 'Pittsburgh Platform of 1885' read 'We recognise in the modern era of universal culture of heart and intellect the approaching of the realisation of Israel's great messianic hope for the establishment of the kingdom of truth, justice and peace among all men. We consider ourselves no longer a nation, but a religious community, and therefore expect neither a return to Palestine, nor a sacrificial worship under the sons of Aaron, nor the restoration of any of the laws concerning the Jewish state.'[5]

However, the rise of antisemitism, bringing a response in the rise of Zionism, and the beginnings of the Shoah already seen in the 1930s, led to a revision of the 'Pittsburgh Platform' in 1937, in Columbus Ohio, where a more positive statement about return to Palestine, the land hallowed by memories and hopes was introduced.

> We affirm the obligation of all Jewry to aid in its upbuilding as a

Jewish homeland...a haven or refuge for the oppressed...This is our messianic goal.[6]

It is obvious that both these descriptions, the Orthodox and the Reform, preclude any idea that Jesus might be the Messiah. However, before we declare, with Rabbi Sylvia Rothschild, that the break is complete, it is important that we consider at least a few of the earlier statements of the Rabbis, for they tell another story.

Let us take, as one key test passage, Isaiah 53, which modern Rabbis, orthodox, reform and liberal, say has no Messianic connotations. Yet we find that Rabbi Moshe El-Sheikh of Safed wrote:

Our rabbis with one voice accept that the prophet is speaking of the King Messiah, and we ourselves shall adhere to the same view.[7]

In the Babylonian Talmud, San 98b, we read:

The Messiah—what is his name?—The rabbis said: His name is 'Leper Scholar' as it is written 'surely he hath borne our griefs and carried our sorrows. Yet we did esteem him a leper, smitten by God and afflicted'.

Rabbi Moshe Kohen ibn Crispin, writing in the middle of the fourteenth century, comments:

The expression 'My Servant' they (certain contemporary commentators) compare rashly with Isaiah 41:8 'thou Israel art my servant'; where the prophet is speaking of the people of Israel: here, however, he does not mention Israel, but simply says 'My Servant': we cannot therefore understand the word in the same sense...I am pleased to interpret it, (ie Isaiah 53) in accordance with the teaching of our Rabbis of King Messiah, and will be careful, so far as I am able, to adhere to the literal sense: thus, possibly, I shall be free from the forced and far-fetched interpretations of which others have been guilty.[8]

These interpretations of Isaiah 53 could be multiplied many times, but there are also other prophetic passages, such as the

Bethlehem prophecy of Micah, which is accepted as Messianic by the ancient rabbis, and which we find fulfilled in the life of Jesus.

The Bethlehem prophecy is especially interesting in that it is accepted as Messianic in the 'Targum Jonathan', written early in the second century CE. Targums have 'long enjoyed a sanctity second only to the Hebrew Text'. To quote Targum Jonathan:

> And you, O Bethlem Ephrath, you who were too small to be numbered among the thousands of the house of Judah, from you shall come forth before Me the Messiah, to exercise dominion over Israel, he whose name was mentioned from before, from the days of creation.[9]

Dr Alfred Edersheim (1825-89), an Austrian Jewish scholar who came to faith in Jesus and joined first the Presbyterian and later the Anglican Ministry, has catalogued in his classic work *The Life and Times of Jesus the Messiah*, over 450 Old Testament passages that were recognised by the ancient Rabbis as prophecies of the Messiah. This whole outlook can be summarised in two Talmudic quotes:

> All the prophets prophesied only for the days of the Messiah (Sanhedrin. 99a).[10]

> The world was created only for the Messiah (Sanhedrin 98b).[11]

Our difficulty is that the Talmud was completed about 500 CE. Very little has survived of Jewish written material during the period of the writing of the New Testament, and the immediate apostolic and early patristic teaching. We cannot therefore know whether the Talmudic quotes authentically represent Jewish tradition in the New Testament period.

The argument therefore between Jesus and the religious leaders of his day was not about whether certain passages in Scripture were Messianic prophecies. The disagreement was rather on the nature of that Messiahship.

When we look at the New Testament, it would seem that on the one hand, there was no idea on the part of the Jewish leadership that the expected Messiah was divine. In fact it was Jesus claim to that position that led to a charge of blasphemy.

'Yes, it is as you say,' Jesus replied. 'But I say to all of you: In the future you will see the Son of Man sitting at the right hand of the Mighty One and coming on the clouds of heaven.' Then the high priest tore his clothes and said, 'He has spoken blasphemy! Why do we need any more witnesses? Look, now you have heard the blasphemy' (Mt 26:64-65).

When Jesus saw their faith, he said, 'Friend, your sins are for-given.' The Pharisees and the teachers of the law began thinking to themselves, 'Who is this fellow who speaks blasphemy? Who can forgive sins but God alone?' (Lk 5:20f).

'We are not stoning you for any of these,' replied the Jews, 'but for blasphemy, because you, a mere man, claim to be God' (John 10:33).

Why then do you accuse me of blasphemy because I said, 'I am God's Son'? (John 10:36)

On the other hand, although there seems to be no concept of the Messiah sharing in the divine nature, there is, in some sections of the Jewish leadership, an appreciation of his eternity, at least into the future, if not from the past.

The crowd spoke up, 'We have heard from the Law that the Christ will remain forever, so how can you say, "The Son of Man must be lifted up"? Who is this "Son of Man"?' (John 12:34).

And what do the ancient rabbis say on this matter? Abraham Ibn Ezra, commenting on Isaiah 9:6 writes:

There are some interpreters who say that 'Wonderful Counsellor, Mighty God, Everlasting Father' are names of God, and only 'Prince of Peace' is the name of the child. But according to my view...all are the names of the child.'[12]

In the face of his own interpretation, Ibn Ezra goes on to take the popular rabbinic view that Isaiah is taking the verse as referring to Hezekiah, suggesting that as Hezekiah would only have been thirty-nine years of age at the period of history he sees it as referring to, he could well be called a child. However, it is clear from its usage in the Hebrew scriptures that 'yeled' consis-tently means 'child', and not 'young man'. We can only conclude that he was trying to avoid the inevitable conclusions of his own deductions as to the real identity of the Messiah.

In the time of Jesus, according to the records in the Talmud, the same debate had already begun, and it was to continue into the present time. Rabbi Hillel had said, 'There shall be no Messiah for Israel, because they have already enjoyed him in the days of Hezekiah.'

Rabbi Joseph said:

> May God forgive him [for saying so]. Now when did Hezekiah flourish? During the first Temple. Yet Zechariah, prophesying in the days of the second, pronounced: Rejoice greatly O daughter of Zion, shout for joy, O daughter of Jerusalem; behold, thy king cometh unto thee! He is just, and having salvation; and riding upon an ass, and upon a colt, the foal of an ass. (Sanhedrin 99a).[13]

On Jeremiah 23:6, Midrash Echa comments:

> What is the name of the King Messiah? To this answered Rabbi Abba bar Kahana: 'Jehovah is his name, for it is written, "This is the name whereby he shall be called—Jehovah Zidkenu".'[14]

THE ISSUES

When we look deeper into the biblical prophecies regarding the Messiah we find that there are, both in the Old Testament and the New Testament, two clearly distinct threads of teaching about the Messiah which appear to give sometimes almost contrary pictures; the Messiah's suffering and sacrifice (eg Isaiah 53) and his sovereignty and eternity (eg Psalm 110).

Christianity has brought these two streams together in the first and second comings of Jesus. He came first in humility to suffer and give his life as an atonement for sin. He will come again in power and glory to judge and to reign.

Judaism has sought to reconcile these by positing two Messiahs, who are described as Messiah Ben Joseph and Messiah Ben David. Messiah Ben Joseph is seen as the first commander of the army in the Messianic wars. Having achieved many great victories he is to die in a great battle in which Israel is defeated by Gog and Magog. His corpse lies in the streets of Jerusalem for forty days, but neither beast nor bird dares to touch it. Then Messiah Ben David comes and brings about the resurrection of his forerunner.

> My son, the Messiah, shall be revealed with those who are with him, and those who remain shall rejoice four hundred years. And after these years my son, the Messiah, shall die, and all who draw breath. And the world shall be turned into primeval silence seven days, as it was at the first beginnings (4 Ezra 7:27-30).[15]

> And the land shall mourn, every family apart (Zech 12:12). Two have interpreted this verse. One said: 'This is the mourning over the Messiah,' and the other said: 'This is the mourning over the Evil Inclination (which will be killed by God in the Messianic days).' (Sukkah 52a).[16]

> The Rabbis have taught: The Holy One, blessed be He, will say to Messiah Ben David, may he be revealed soon in our days! 'Ask of Me anything, and I will give it to you, for it is written, "The Lord said unto me, Thou art My son, this day I have begotten thee, ask of Me and I will give thee the nations for thy inheritance (Ps 2:7-8)." And when he will see that Messiah Ben Joseph will be slain, he will say before Him "Master of the world! I ask nothing of you except life!" God will say to him "Even before you said 'life' your father David prophesied about you, as it is written, 'He asked life of Thee, Thou gavest it him.' " ' (Ps 21:4) (Sukkah 52a).[17]

We must beware of reading too much into the resurrection account of the slain Messiah Ben Joseph. The thought here is of bringing back to life, in the way that the widow's son was brought back to life, and others were brought back to life in the Jewish Scriptures. It would be reading too much into the text to see Messiah Ben David as 'type' of Jesus. Nevertheless it is clear that the fuller doctrine of resurrection is not alien to rabbinic thinking, and is central to the New Testament expectation.

> the gospel he promised beforehand through his prophets in the Holy Scriptures regarding his Son, who as to his human nature was a descendant of David, and who through the Spirit of holiness was declared with power to be the Son of God by his resurrection from the dead: Jesus Christ our Lord (Rom 1:2-4).

Paul is not saying that Jesus' resurrection changed his status. It didn't make him Son of God or Messiah. It declared, made evident and open for all to see who Jesus was. The focus of New Testament preaching, in the ministry of Jesus, Peter and Paul, is that the resurrection is the final affirmation for the identity of Jesus as Messiah and Son of God. Like so many fulfilments of prophecy, the nature of that fulfilment only becomes clear after the event; but once it is seen it becomes assuredly clear.

The Midrashim on Psalm 16:9 and the whole of Psalm 110 see the texts as messianic.[18]

Jesus confronts the two disciples on the Emmaus Road and says:

> 'How foolish you are, and how slow of heart to believe all that the prophets have spoken! Did not the Christ have to suffer these things and then enter his glory?' And beginning with Moses and all the Prophets, he explained to them what was said in all the Scriptures concerning himself (Lk 24:25-27).

After their recognition of who he was they confessed, 'Were not our hearts burning within us while he talked with us on the road and opened the Scriptures to us?' (Lk 24:32).

This has considerable bearing on the Church's traditional attitude that the Jews have been rejected for killing Jesus. That this cannot be sustained is seen first from the prayer of Jesus himself, when he said, 'Father, forgive them, for they do not know what they are doing.' (Lk 23:34). And Peter, after the healing of the crippled beggar by the temple gate, makes it quite clear that the way the Jews handled Jesus was done in ignorance and was atoned for, and covered by the prayer of Jesus.

> When Peter saw this, he said to them: 'Men of Israel, why does this surprise you? Why do you stare at us as if by our own power or godliness we had made this man walk? The God of Abraham, Isaac and Jacob, the God of our fathers, has glorified his servant Jesus. You handed him over to be killed, and you disowned him before Pilate, though he had decided to let him go. You disowned the Holy and Righteous One and asked that a murderer be released to you. You killed the author of life, but God raised him from the dead. We are witnesses of this. By faith in the name of

Jesus, this man whom you see and know was made strong. It is Jesus' name and the faith that comes through him that has given this complete healing to him, as you can all see. 'Now, brothers, I know that you acted in ignorance, as did your leaders. But this is how God fulfilled what he had foretold through all the prophets, saying that his Christ would suffer. Repent, then, and turn to God, so that your sins may be wiped out, that times of refreshing may come from the Lord, and that he may send the Christ, who has been appointed for you—even Jesus. He must remain in heaven until the time comes for God to restore everything, as he promised long ago through his holy prophets. For Moses said, 'The Lord your God will raise up for you a prophet like me from among your own people; you must listen to everything he tells you. Anyone who does not listen to him will be completely cut off from among his people.' 'Indeed, all the prophets from Samuel on, as many as have spoken, have foretold these days. And you are heirs of the prophets and of the covenant God made with your fathers. He said to Abraham, 'Through your offspring all peoples on earth will be blessed.' When God raised up his servant, he sent him first to you to bless you by turning each of you from your wicked ways.' (Acts 3:12-26).

The point of Peter's message is: 'Yes, you handed him over...you disowned him...you killed him...' in all these things you acted in ignorance. These things have been atoned for and covered by the prayer of Jesus.

They had seen in this healing the evidence for the resurrection, and in that, the evidence for Jesus' Messianic claims. The challenge to the Jews therefore was not so much to repent for the death of Jesus, but rather to repent (literally to change their minds, which is what repentance means) regarding their unbelief about the evidence for the resurrection.

In Romans 11:20 it now becomes clear that 'unbelief' has less (or rather nothing) to do with the death of Jesus, and everything to do with his resurrection, an unbelief which Gentiles also share in, until their eyes are opened by hearing and responding to the Gospel. If this had been clearly appreciated from the beginning of church history, nearly two thousand years of deep pain in Christian-Jewish relationships could have been avoided.

Was the 'two Messiah' theory in existence during the time of Jesus ministry? This question is probably impossible to answer because the Talmud was not completed until about 500 CE; in fact there is almost no other literature available which covers Jewish life and thinking in New Testament times, other than the New Testament itself. But let us look at Matthew's account of Jesus entry into Jerusalem, and compare it with the Zechariah prophecy that lies behind it.

> As they approached Jerusalem and came to Bethphage on the Mount of Olives, Jesus sent two disciples, saying to them, 'Go to the village ahead of you, and at once you will find a donkey tied there, with her colt by her. Untie them and bring them to me. If anyone says anything to you, tell him that the Lord needs them, and he will send them right away.' This took place to fulfil what was spoken through the prophet: 'Say to the Daughter of Zion, "See, your king comes to you, gentle and riding on a donkey, on a colt, the foal of a donkey." ' The disciples went and did as Jesus had instructed them. They brought the donkey and the colt, placed their cloaks on them, and Jesus sat on them. A very large crowd spread their cloaks on the road, while others cut branches from the trees and spread them on the road. The crowds that went ahead of him and those that followed shouted, 'Hosanna to the Son of David!' 'Blessed is he who comes in the name of the Lord!' 'Hosanna in the highest!' When Jesus entered Jerusalem, the whole city was stirred and asked, 'Who is this?' The crowds answered, 'This is Jesus, the prophet from Nazareth in Galilee.' (Mt 21:1-11).

> Rejoice greatly, O Daughter of Zion! Shout, Daughter of Jerusalem! See, your king comes to you, righteous and having salvation, gentle and riding on a donkey, on a colt, the foal of a donkey. I will take away the chariots from Ephraim and the war-horses from Jerusalem, and the battle bow will be broken. He will proclaim peace to the nations. His rule will extend from sea to sea and from the River to the ends of the earth. (Zech 9:9f).

Zechariah 9:9 speaks of a king coming in humility, and chapter 9:10 of the triumphant removal of the occupying enemy from Jerusalem. Because Jesus was dramatically fulfilling the first, the people were expectantly waiting for him to fulfil the second. In their thinking the two deeds hung together as the work of one and the same person. The idea of two Messiahs does not seem to have been in their thoughts and was probably not current in Jesus' time. Possibly it became part of the Jewish hope as a result of the destruction of the Temple and Jerusalem in CE 70 and 134.

The New Testament does not lend support to the 'two Messiah' theory, but Jesus, in both his teaching and practice has fulfilled some of the Messianic prophecies and shows in his teaching, in sufficient outline, though not in clear detail, how he will fulfil the rest.

The breach between Christian and current rabbinic views regarding the Messiah are, humanly speaking, unbridgeable. What we have shown is that there was, in the teaching of the ancient Rabbis, an understanding of the Messianic prophecies with which the New Testament fulfilment in Jesus is not in conflict. As Jews we can therefore rightly claim to stand in the blood line and covenant relationship of our forefather Abraham. As followers of Yeshua ha Mashiach (Hebrew for Jesus the Messiah—common terminology amongst Messianic Jews), whose life and ministry was prophesied in the Tanach and fulfilled in the Brit hadashah, we also stand in the tradition accepted and developed by some of the most respected of our ancient rabbis. We can therefore lay claim to the title Messianic Judaism with full integrity.

There is one other fundamental difference regarding the coming of the Messiah we cannot ignore, and that is regarding the conditions and reasons of his coming. Rabbi Yechiel Eckstein, commenting on the Jewish doctrine of 'tikkun olam', or 'fixing the world', which, he says, has become widely accepted (in Judaism) in recent years, writes about the coming of the Messiah thus:

> To a large degree it is man, through his actions, who can either bring the Messiah and the age of redemption or delay their arrival. According to the Midrash, the Messiah waits in heaven, eager to enter the world as soon as all people become either righteous (ie as a reward) or sinners (ie when redemption from a source outside of man becomes necessary to fulfil God's covenant and promise of redemption). In either case, it is man's actions that can bring the Messiah, complete the world, and redeem the universe. God needs man, his co-partner in the building of this earth, to achieve these goals.[19]

Incidentally we find in this midrash further support for a

'more than human' view of the Messiah, someone who pre-exists his coming into the world, at least reminiscent of the words of Jesus, 'Before Abraham was born, I am.' (John 8:58).

More fundamentally we see here a very wrong kind of exaltation of the human power to affect (or at least to 'timetable') God's purposes, which to us seems contrary to the clear teaching of Scriptures concerning God's sovereign decision in this matter.

> When the time had fully come, God sent his Son, born of a woman, born under law, that we might receive the full rights of sons. Because you are sons, God sent the Spirit of his Son into our hearts, the Spirit who calls out 'Abba, Father'... (Gal 4:4-6).

This all seems to be related to the rabbinic watering down of the doctrine of sin, the results of the fall since the destruction of the Temple and the concomitant abolition of the sacrifices.

We would affirm that God has, in his sovereign grace, freely chosen man to be a co-partner to achieve his goals. We would deny that God needs man. We would further affirm that man's place in being a co-partner depends first on his being willing to admit his fallen helplessness, his need of redemption through the atoning sacrifice of Jesus, and the infilling of the Holy Spirit, before he can take the place that Judaism, as it seems to us, too quickly ascribes to him.

It is clear that a great variety of views regarding the identity of the Messiah have been expressed, and are acceptable, within the breadth of Jewish belief through the ages. The one view that is not acceptable, and is avoided at all costs, is that Jesus could be the Messiah.

CHAPTER 19

What on Earth is God doing?

THE QUESTION IS NOT MEANT to be irreverent. Nor, alas, is it original.

I am frequently asked just what is the point and purpose of Messianic Judaism? My only answer is that our very existence arises out of our desire to be faithful to the purposes of God as revealed in Scripture to the best of our ability.

We acknowledge that there is one body and one Spirit, one hope, one Lord, one faith, one baptism (Eph 4:4f). This includes and unites Jewish and Gentiles believers in Jesus.

We acknowledge that there is only one way of salvation, and that is through faith in the atoning death of Jesus, and his glorious resurrection.

We acknowledge that there is only one bride, and therefore the bride of Isaiah 62 and Ephesians 5 must be the same.

We acknowledge the high priestly prayer of Jesus in John 17, that his people might be one, and we have no desire for schism in the body. We do not see ourselves in the manner of denominational divisiveness, though we may not always be guiltless of that kind of attitude.

We do not see Messianic Judaism as having a continuing existence in the age to come, heaven, life after death, or whatever we may wish to call it. When the bride of Christ is perfected, it may well do away with all distinctive expressions of faith and life within the body.

We believe the following statements to be biblical and therefore true, at least for the present age. What on earth is God doing?

1. God, as a sign of his covenant faithfulness, and the immutability of his promises, has purposed that the Jewish people will survive as an identifiable people, as long as the sun and the moon endure.

2. God has purposed that this Jewish survival is guaranteed by reason of a continuing remnant of faith in their midst. We believe that, by the grace of God, we are that remnant, and therefore we would be unfaithful, both to God and to our people, if we did not maintain that identity, not only in our social life, but also in our worship and spiritual identity.

3. God has sent to the Jewish people a Messiah, a prophet, priest and king, who is Yeshua haMashiach, and who, through the testimony of Jewish believers was to be revealed as Saviour of the world.

4. We believe that God, who is himself plurality in unity, reflects that same quality in humankind, which is, after all, created in his image. This is as true in the Jew/Gentile distinctive as it is in the male/female distinctive.

It is not without significance that Maimonides, in the second of his Thirteen Principles of Faith, (I believe with perfect faith that the Creator, blessed be his name, is a Unity, and that there is no unity in any manner like unto his...)[1], changes the Hebrew 'Echad', which admits the understanding of organic and corporate unity, to 'Yachid', which signifies mathematical, solitary unity. It is highly probable that at least part of the purpose behind his thinking was anti-Trinitarian polemic, but he could not achieve this without changing the plain language of his own Scriptures.

Distinctives within the one body, as long as they are complementary, and not competitive or divisive, are not wrong, and can be positively beneficial in achieving the fullness of the purposes of God.

We recognise that the resurgence of such a movement as Messianic Judaism within the body of Messiah can seem threatening to the long established Church. We recognise how this must seem, and we repent that we are not always free of the sin of pride. However we have to point out that the now mainly Gentile Church is not complete in itself without us. We need one another, but without either of us losing our own distinctiveness.

In regarding ourselves as 'Messianic' Jewish, we do not recognise ourselves as just one more movement within the 'Rabbinic' Jewish community of faith, as though we were one more variety of choice alongside the orthodox, reform, liberal etc. We believe that we stand in the direct line of biblical Judaism.

When the Jewish community began to exclude those of its

members who expressed faith in Yeshua, it wandered off the line of God's truth.

When the Church began to insist that its Jewish members 'assimilate', and lay aside their Jewishness, it also wandered off the line of God's truth.

What on earth is God doing? He is bringing both back to the centre line of his purposes through a new understanding of his purposes in Yeshua, and in so doing he is reuniting those who should never have become divided.

Our challenge to the rabbinic leadership of the Jewish community, and to the community as a whole, is to be willing to openly re-evaluate the evidence for Jesus' Messiahship without being deflected by the history of Christian antisemitism. These are separate issues, and the confusion of the two inevitably leads to a blindness to the truth.

Our challenge to the church is to recognise its Jewish roots and to allow that recognition to permeate its theology, its structures, and its whole way of thinking and living.

Christians often say to me that they recognise the Jewish roots of the Church, but when we discuss this further it becomes clear that they recognise the Jewishness, not as roots, but as a seed. I am not splitting hairs: the difference is vital. When a plant grows from a seed, the seed is decisive as to the nature of the plant, but the seed 'dies'; it plays no further part in the life of the plant. In the case of a plant and its roots, the plant, however mature it becomes, can have no separate existence if detached from its roots: and neither can the roots without the remainder of the plant. There is an organic unity between the two in which neither part can continue to exist for long without the other.

What would such a recognition mean for the Church? It would mean a major re-alignment regarding its understanding of its own history. If that seems nebulous I will give a few practical illustrations and suggestions.

At the enthronement of Archbishop George Carey great care was taken to invite representatives, both of the present breadth of the Church's life and of its historic beginnings. There were many representatives of early middle Eastern Orthodox Churches, yet there was no representative of where it all started, the Jewish Church.

In the historic Councils of the Church, at least from Nicea to the present day, no leader from the Jewish Churches has been invited as a delegate. In fact, it is hard not to draw the conclusion that there is something of a conspiracy of exclusion, though of course these things are by nature almost impossible to prove. Also in those places where there is a dialogue between Jews and Christians, both parties to the dialogue agree to prevent the participation of Messianic Jews, and wherever Jewish-Christian relations are on the agenda, Messianic Jews are not consulted or given an opportunity to express a viewpoint. These are not the actions of a Church that now seeks to affirm its Jewish roots!

A Church that takes its Jewish roots seriously will be willing to rethink its traditional interpretation of the 'Acts of the Apostles', especially the decisions of the Council of Jerusalem, and the way these things are seen as worked out in Paul's letters to the Christians in Rome and Galatia. It is no longer tenable to take the simplistic view that Jewish Christianity (I use the title most frequently used by historians) degenerated into the Ebionite sect (from the Hebrew 'Ebionim'–poor men), one of the groups of Jewish Christians which died out after the destruction of the temple and the sacking of Jerusalem. This group developed a reduced doctrine of the Person of Jesus, in that they taught that he was the natural son of Joseph and Mary. Whilst we may accept that this group fell into error, the evidence that this took with it the whole, or even the main group of Jewish believers in Jesus is simply not there.

All too frequently it is assumed that the main line of division in the apostolic Church was the 'Jewish-Christian' line led by the extremists in Jerusalem, and the 'mainstream' Church led by Paul. It is then assumed that after the destruction of Temple and Jerusalem, the influence of the 'Jewish-Christian' stream died out, and the mainly Gentile Church came into the ascendancy. The latter fact cannot be denied, but the reasons are not as given. From the Council of Jerusalem there is no shred of evidence that there was a split between Paul and the mainstream leaders of the Jewish Church. In fact they went to considerable lengths to scotch rumours falsely put about, that Paul was creating such a split.

They have been informed that you teach all the Jews who live among the Gentiles to turn away from Moses, telling them not to circumcise their children or live according to our customs. What shall we do? They will certainly hear that you have come, so do what we tell you. There are four men with us who have made a vow. Take these men, join in their purification rites and pay their expenses, so that they can have their heads shaved. Then everybody will know there is no truth in these reports about you, but that you yourself are living in obedience to the law. (Acts 21:21-24)

When we ask how these ideas came about it becomes clear that the mainstream of Jewish Christianity, of which both James and Paul are representatives, (Paul can be confidently included even with his call to Gentile Church planting) did not simply fall into Ebionite heresy. Mainstream Jewish Christianity fell into eclipse, first by reason of the pressure of exclusion from the Jewish leadership on the one hand, and the increasingly predominantly Gentile leadership on the other. Jewish pressure came after the failure of the Bar Kochba revolt from which Messianic Jews had withdrawn after Bar Kochba had been declared the Messiah by Rabbi Achiva. Gentile Christian pressure came because of increasing political expediency in the Roman Empire for not being tied to a Jewish identity. Professor James Dunn writes in 'The Parting of the Ways':

In the second century the problem (of the parting of the ways between Christianity and Judaism) was compounded with the steadily emerging sense of Christians as a third race–Jews as well as Gentiles becoming 'them' to the Christian 'us', Christianity as alone the true Israel. The other and tragic side of this emergence of a clear and distinctive Christian identity was the steady growth of antisemitism. It is and remains a deeply disturbing fact that catholic Christianity found it necessary to define itself against Judaism, all too often by vilifying Jews–in the early centuries most disturbingly in Chrysostom's 'Homily Against the Jews'. Here was a great irony: Christianity began by rejecting the ethnocentricity of Judaism and Jewish Christianity; but in coming to think of itself as a separate 'race', it opened the door to a different kind of racialism, where Christians defined themselves by excluding 'the Jews', making the very mistake against which Paul in particular protested so vehemently.[2]

However, looking to the future, Dunn continues,

> Does the period from before the parting of the ways provide us with resources for present and future which will enable us to recover more of that earlier continuity and to rediscover that character of earliest Christian mission as a movement for renewal within the Judaism of the time?
>
> The increasing number of Messianic Jews...offer fresh bridging possibilities, since the Jew/Christian spectrum is more complete now than at any time since the early decades when Jewish Christianity was a vital option.

But for Dunn the start of this journey of recovery of that earlier continuity depends on the fulfilment of certain conditions, and his 'map' for that journey, though leaving plenty of opportunity for discovery, nevertheless has certain fixed points, which he sees as non-negotiable.

> The unity between the historical Jesus and the exalted Christ, that is to say, the conviction that the charismatic preacher from Nazareth had ministered, died and been raised from the dead to bring God and man finally together, the recognition that the divine power through which they now worshipped and were encountered and accepted by God was one and the same person, Jesus, the man, the Christ, the Son of God, the Lord, the life-giving Spirit.[3]

In the present time there is a crisis of confidence in the Church regarding a clear presentation of Jesus as the Messiah, Saviour and Lord for Jew and Gentile alike. Dialogue, with a view towards mutual understanding, acceptance, respect and support are the order of the day. We do not wish to denigrate any of those sentiments: they are truly praiseworthy and warrant our support. But the kind of dialogue which is limited to these things does not go far enough. The ultimate aim of dialogue must be a sharing of beliefs, insights, understandings etc, with a view to coming to the truth. In the matter of the Jewish-Christian relationship, it is God's plan, not just that we accept and respect one another, but that through faith in Jesus we might become one. We hope that, with one pier on each bank, we Messianic Jews might become a bridge. Bridges are designed to be walked over, even if that sometimes feels like being trampled on.

Notes

Chapter 1

1. The Torah readings are from the Pentateuch. The HafTorah, from the rest of the Hebrew Scriptures. Brit haDashah is Hebrew for 'New Covenant'.
2. Siddur. The authorised Daily Prayer Book of the Ashkenazi (European background) Jews. The Prayer Book of the Sephardi (Oriental background) Jews is called the Tephillah.
3. Halakah. The legal part of talmudic and later Jewish literature, referring especially to the Oral Law, the accepted tradition of interpretation of the written law.
4. Profession of Faith, from the Church of Constantinople. As cited in Michael Shiffman, *The Return of the Remnant* (Lederer Publications: Baltimore), p 39.

Chapter 2

1. As quoted by Rev Eric Gabe, *The Hebrew Christian Magazine* (Series beginning 1987) vol 2.
2. *Ibid*
3. The Church's Ministry among the Jews was founded in 1809 as The London Society for Promoting Christianity amongst the Jews.
4. Dr C.G. Barth, *History of the London Society for Promoting Christianity amongst the Jews* (L.S.P.C.J.: London, 1908), p 42.
5. Lewis Way, *Memoirs on the State of the Israelites*. Dedicated and Presented to their Imperial and Royal Majesties Assembled at the Aix-La-Chapelle Congress (1819). French copy in the British Library. English translation by Claud Bonjour (not published).
6. Lewis Way's 175th anniversary memorial service. From introduction to order of service, by Penelope Swift. Not otherwise published.

Chapter 8

1. H.C.G. Moule, *Romans*, The Classic New Testament Commentary (Marshall Pickering: London, 1992), p 206.
2. Tom Wright, *Jerusalem in the New Testament*, Ed. P.W.L Walker (Tyndale House: Cambridge, 1992), p 65.
3. *Ibid*, p 67.
4. James Dunn, *Romans*, Word Biblical Commentary (Dallas, Texas: 1991), p 658.
5. *Ibid*, p 691.
6. Chris Wright, *Jerusalem Past and Present in the Purposes of God*, p 18.

7. *Study Bible*, New International Version (Hodder & Stoughton: 1987).
8. Arnold Fruchtenbaum, *Hebrew Christianity* (Ariel Press: San Antonio, Texas, 1983), p 21.

Chapter 10
1. Midrash. Rabbinic comment. The finding of new meaning, in addition to the literal one, in the Scriptures. Talmudic tradition has formulated certain rules to deduce such hidden and new meanings.

Chapter 14
1. Babylonian Talmud. Soncino Edition. Sotah 22b. p 112.

Chapter 16
1. Yechiel Eckstein, *What Christians Should Know about Jews and Judaism* (Word Books: Waco, Texas, 1984), p 65f.
2. *The New Union Haggadah*, Central Conference of American Rabbis, Second Revised Edition (Penguin Books: New York, 1982), p 78.
3. Abraham Heschel, quoted by Yechiel Eckstein. *Op. cit.* p 66.
4. *Midrash Rabbah*, vol 1. (Soncino Press: London, 1977), Translated by Dr. H. Freudman, p 68.
5. Babylonian Talmud (*Op. cit.*) Yoma 69b. p 328.
6. Authorised Prayer Book (*Op. cit.*) p 193.
7. Michael Friedlander, *The Jewish Religion*, 1913, p 417. As quoted in the Jewish Encyclopedia section on 'Sacrifice'. p 615.
8. Babylonian Talmud. (*Op. cit.*) Shabbat 146a. p 738.
9. *Op. cit.* Footnote to 8.
10. Dan Cohn-Sherbok. 'Why Today's Society Needs to Reconsider the Forgotten Doctrine of Original Sin', *Church of England Newspaper* (26th March 1993).

Chapter 18
1. Authorised Prayer Book. (*Op. cit.*) p 95.
2. Shmuel Arkush, Founder of 'Operation Judaism' 1986. Sponsored by the Office of the Chief Rabbi and Board of Deputies of British Jews. As quoted in the 'Heart of the Matter' series–'King of the Jews?' Easter Sunday 1991.
3. *Ibid*
4. Encyclopaedia Judaica, Section on *Messiah*, p 1408 (Kefer Publishing House: Jerusalem, 1972).
5. *Op. cit.* p 1415.
6. *Op. cit.* p 1415.
7. Rabbi Moshe El-Sheikh of Safed, *Commentaries of the Earlier Prophets* (Late 16th century), p 258.
8. *The Suffering Servant of Isaiah According to the Jewish Interpreters* (vol 2), S.R. Driver and A. Neubauer (Hermon Press: New York, 1877), reprinted (1969), pp 99,100.

9. Targum Jonathan on Micah 5:2 *ad. loc.* Jerusalem (Hebrew) Edition. (Deyfus: 1961), p 195.

10. Babylonian Talmud. (*Op. cit.*) Sanhedrin 99a. p 670.

11. *Op. cit.* p 667.

12. *The Commentary of Ibn Ezra on Isaiah 9:6, ad. loc.,* Translated by Dr M. Friedlander (Philipp Feldheim: New York, 1873), pp 51,52.

13. Babylonian Talmud. (*Op. cit.*) Sanhedrin 99a. p 669.

14. Midrash on Jeremiah 23:6 *ad. loc. Midrash Rabbah* (vol 4) (*Op. cit.*) p 134.

15. 4 Ezra 7:27-30, *The Old Testament Pseudepigrapha,* Ed. J.H. Charlesworth (Darton Longman and Todd: Vol 1, London, 1983), p 537.

16. Babylonian Talmud. (*Op. cit.*) Sukkah 52a. p 246.

17. *Ibid* p 247.

18. Edersheim (*Op. cit.*) List of O.T. Passages Messianically Applied in Rabbinic Writings. Appendix IX.

19. Eckstein (*Op. cit.*) p 78.

Chapter 19

1. Authorised Prayer Book. (*Op. cit.*) p 93.

2. J.D.G. Dunn, *The Parting of the Ways* (SCM Press: London, 1991), p 248.

3. *Op. cit.* p 249.